מַעֲרָכָה

ArtScroll Youth Series®

A Story

by G. Sofer

translated by
Shaindel Weinbach

illustrated by
Miriam Bardugo

Stories from our history and heritage,
from ancient times to modern times,
arranged according to the Jewish calendar.

Published by

Mesorah Publications, ltd

in conjunction with

 **SAPIR /**
Jerusalem

FIRST EDITION
First Impression . . . September, 1989

Published and Distributed by
MESORAH PUBLICATIONS, Ltd.
Brooklyn, New York 11232

Distributed in Israel by
MESORAH MAFITZIM / J. GROSSMAN
Rechov Harav Uziel 117
Jerusalem, Israel

Distributed in Europe by
J. LEHMANN HEBREW BOOKSELLERS
20 Cambridge Terrace
Gateshead, Tyne and Wear
England NE8 1RP

Distributed in Australia & New Zealand by
GOLD'S BOOK & GIFT CO.
36 William Street
Balaclava 3183, Vic., Australia

Distributed in South Africa by
KOLLEL BOOKSHOP
22 Muller Street
Yeoville 2198, South Africa

THE ARTSCROLL YOUTH SERIES®
A STORY A DAY I: Tishrei-Cheshvan
© Copyright 1989, by MESORAH PUBLICATIONS, Ltd.
4401 Second Avenue / Brooklyn, N.Y. 11232 / (718) 921-9000

ISBN:
0-89906-950-9 (hard cover)
0-89906-951-7 (paperback)

Typography by CompuScribe at ArtScroll Studios, Ltd.

Printed in the United States of America by Noble Book Press Corp.
Bound by Sefercraft, Quality Bookbinders, Ltd. Brooklyn, N.Y.

ೈ§ Table of Contents

Tishrei

Cheshvan

Tishrei

Rosh Hashanah. This is the birthday of man, the day on which Adam was created and received his eternal soul from the Almighty. This day was established as the beginning of the year, *Rosh Hashanah*, a day of judgment for all mankind.

Only Flesh and Blood

Hadrian, the Roman emperor, conquered the entire world. Upon returning from his military campaigns, he said to his ministers, "I demand that you worship me as a god, for the entire world belongs to me!"

"If so," said one of his wise ministers, "I need your help."

"What is troubling you?" asked Hadrian, the mighty conqueror.

"I have a ship at sea. I have invested my entire fortune in it, but it is about to sink. What shall I do? I will be left penniless if that ship is not saved."

"Fear not," Hadrian assured him. "I will send my fleet to save the sinking ship and its cargo."

"Why go to such trouble?" asked the clever minister, in mock surprise. "All you need do is dispatch a mighty wind to speed the ship to land. Then all will be easily saved."

"How can I send a wind to your ship?"

"You cannot tell the wind what to do? Then how do you expect people to worship you as a powerful god?"

Hadrian scowled angrily at this question, but did not reply. He retired to his palace, sullen and displeased.

His wife said, "You are a mighty king; everything is in your power. If you wish to be a god, nothing can deter you. But there is one thing you must do first: Return the deposit to the Almighty, then you can become a god yourself."

"To what deposit are you referring?" he asked.

"Your soul."

"And what can I do without a soul? I will be lifeless, unable to do a thing!"

"If you are not the master of your own soul," said the clever woman, "how can you expect to be a god? Admit it; you are a mere mortal!"

2 Tishrei

This is the second day of *Rosh Hashanah*.

Let Every Creation Know

The disciples of the *Maggid* of Mezeritch would visit their master on *Rosh Hashanah* eve to hear his warm words of inspiration.

One year, the *Maggid* did not expound Torah as always, to everyone's surprise. The chasidim noticed that their youngest comrade, R' Shneur Zalman of Liady, was missing and they understood that the *Maggid* was awaiting his arrival before he began his Torah discourse.

They sought R' Shneur Zalman and found him in the *beis medrash*. There he stood, grasping his wooden *shtender* (lectern) tightly, and shouting at the top of his voice, "Oh, let every creature know that You have created it!" — a line from the *shemoneh esrei*; R' Shneur Zalman had not yet finished his prayers.

They waited patiently for him to conclude and then led him to the *Maggid*.

The *Maggid* knew the reason for the delay and said, "When R' Shneur Zalman utters the words 'Let every creature know that You have created it,' he does not budge from the spot until even his wooden *shtender* acknowledges that 'You have created it'!"

Breaking the Barriers

Shortly before *Rosh Hashanah*, the Baal Shem Tov told his favorite disciple, R' Ze'ev Kitzes, that he, R' Ze'ev, was to blow the *shofar* that year. "But you must first study the deeper meanings of the *tekiyos* as spelled out by the sages of Kabbalah."

R' Ze'ev threw himself into the study of *kavanos*, the profound intentions of the mystics which one should have in mind when blowing the *shofar*. He even wrote them down, intending to have the sheet on which they were written before him, while blowing.

The day of *Rosh Hashanah* arrived, and the long-awaited moment of the blowing of the *shofar*. R' Ze'ev fumbled in his pocket for his notes but the paper had disappeared! He searched everywhere, but the paper had vanished. He felt terrible, because without those notes, he would not remember upon what to concentrate while he blew for the congregation! He would not remember the holy *kavanos* of the *Zohar*! His heart sank at the thought of his worthlessness and he burst into bitter tears.

There was nothing for him to do but proceed and he decided to blow the *shofar* while thinking of the obvious, simple meanings represented by the *shofar*. He concentrated deeply upon the concept, "I am about to fulfill the commandment of my Creator, Who ordered me to blow the *shofar* on this day." This was the only thought which filled his mind while he blew that day in the Baal Shem Tov's *beis medrash*.

At the conclusion of the service, the Baal Shem Tov turned to him and said, "The celestial palaces each have a separate key, but there is a way to open up all the gates at one and the same time, and that is with an axe.

"The *kavanos*, the deep mystical thoughts which our sages, the *mekubalim*, taught us, are the individual keys to each Heavenly palace. But a broken, downtrodden heart is the mighty axe which, with one blow, can break through all of the barriers!"

This is the Fast of Gedalyah. Some two months after the destruction of the *Beis Hamikdash*, Gedalyah ben Achikam, the leader of the remnant of Jewry in Jerusalem, was slain. This occurred in 3309 (451 B.C.E.).

Our Sages wished to commemorate this day for all time and established the Fast of Gedalyah on the third of *Tishrei (Rosh Hashanah 18b and Rashi)*.

In the Footsteps of the Exiles

Gedalyah ben Achikam was appointed by Neb-uchadnezzar as the leader of the remnant of Jewry in Judea. But Yishmael ben Nesanyah, who could not bear his rule, rose up and murdered him in cold blood.

The remnant of Jews fled to Egypt, taking along with them Yirmeyahu the prophet and his disciple, Baruch ben Neriyah, who had stayed behind after most of Jewry were exiled to Babylonia. Now, after their departure, the land was completely desolate.

☙ ☙ ☙

Yirmeyahu, one of the greatest of our prophets, exhorted the people to repent of their sinful ways before the destruction of the *Beis Hamikdash.* He warned them that their sins would lead to the destruction.

Yirmeyahu wrote part of *Eichah* (Lamentations), in which he mourned the destruction of the *Beis Hamikdash* and of Jerusalem even before the *churban.* Later, when the destruction became a reality, he completed *Eichah.*

Yirmeyahu's merit protected Jerusalem all the years. As long as he was in the city, the enemy could not destroy it. But on the day that he left and his presence no longer protected it, the city was laid waste, along with the *Beis Hamikdash.*

Upon his return, Yirmeyahu saw the city in ruins and the *Beis Hamikdash* in flames. "Where did the exiles go?" he cried. "What direction did they take? Show me, so that I may go with them."

He wandered until he found a bloodstained path and followed it until he overtook the exiles. He ran up to them and hugged them and kissed them. He cried and they cried. "This has befallen you," he said, "for not having taken heed of my words."

They continued on, urged forward by their captors, until they reached the banks of the Euphrates. Nevuzaradan turned to Yirmeyahu and said, "Do you wish to come with us to Babylonia?" Yirmeyahu mulled this over in his mind and said, "If I join the exiles, there will be no one to comfort those who remain behind in Jerusalem." He parted from them and returned to his beloved city to console the remnant there.

For the Sake of Wood and Stones

Yirmeyahu returned sadly to Jerusalem. When he beheld the *Beis Hamikdash* in its destruction, he fell upon the wood and stones, and burst into bitter tears.

Just then, the famous Greek philosopher Plato passed by. Plato saw a man weeping and asked a passerby, "Who is that man?"

"A Jewish sage," he was told.

Plato approached the prophet and said, "They say that you are a wise man. Tell me, why do you weep over these ruins of wood and stone?"

Yirmeyahu replied, "And they say that you, too, are a great philosopher. Do you have any questions that disturb you?"

"Yes," admitted the thinker. "I have questions, but I don't believe that there is anyone who can answer them."

"Ask them, regardless," said Yirmeyahu. "I will answer them."

Plato posed his questions and Yirmeyahu answered them all, one by one.

The Greek philosopher was deeply impressed by the wisdom of the Jewish sage and asked, "How did you acquire such a wealth of knowledge?"

"From these very sticks and stones," replied Yirmeyahu sadly.

The fourth of the Ten Days of Penitence.

Worthy of Miracles

*T*eshuvah, repentance, of itself, is not sufficient to wipe away sins that a person has committed against his fellow man. He must first approach that person, appease him and receive forgiveness. It is, therefore, customary during the Days of Penitence that each one asks forgiveness from others, for fear that one may have wronged a friend without realizing it.

If a person is aware that he has sinned against another, he must make every effort to appease him and receive his pardon.

And if a person has, indeed, been wronged or insulted, he should not be cruel and hard hearted, but forgiving and kind. He should accept his friend's apology and pardon him at once.

❀　❀　❀

Our Sages tell us that R' Abba was once sitting by the gates of Lod, when he saw a man returning from a journey. Tottering with exhaustion, the traveler entered a ruin, settled himself against a wall which seemed about to collapse and was soon sound asleep.

R' Abba noticed a snake slipping out of its hole. It approached the sleeping man and was about to bite. Before R'

Abba could even cry out in alarm, a creature pounced upon the snake and killed it.

The man slept innocently on. He awoke some time later, refreshed, and looked about him. There, a few feet from him, lay the body of the poisonous snake. Not realizing how close he had been to death, the man rose and continued on.

The moment he reached the road, the walls of the ruins caved in, falling on the very spot where he had lain so peacefully before.

R' Abba could not believe his eyes and could no longer contain himself. He ran to the traveler and asked, "Who are you? What do you do? Do you know that your life has been miraculously saved twice this morning? Why have you deserved these two miracles?"

The man replied, "I have never borne anyone a grudge. Whenever a person wronged or hurt me and came to apologize, I always forgave him. And even if it happened that I was not reconciled immediately, I would not go to sleep until I had forgiven him. Furthermore, from that time on, I made a special effort to be kind to him and win his affection."

"Indeed!" cried R' Abba, "You surely are worthy to have the Holy One perform miracle after miracle for you."

With tears gathering in his eyes, he added, "Your deeds are greater than Yosef's. Yosef forgave his brothers for what they did to him. But that is natural, for they were his flesh and blood. But you forgive everyone, even if they are not related. Truly, you are greater than Yosef!" (*Zohar Mikeitz*)

Forgiveness — Fifteen Years Later

*I*t is said that R' Akiva Eiger never became angry at anyone — never, that is, except once.

He was then the head of a large *yeshivah* in Lisa. He learned that one of his students did not behave as a *yeshivah* student should. R' Akiva summoned the boy to his home and, when it became evident that the information was correct, R' Akiva became very angry and ordered the student to leave the *yeshivah* immediately.

Fifteen years passed. R' Akiva had left Lisa and was now rabbi of Friedland.

One day he learned that that young man was living in Breslau. As soon as he heard that, R' Akiva wrote him a letter.

"Fifteen years ago," he wrote, "when you were a student of mine in Lisa, I lost my temper and shouted at you. I have never forgiven myself since, and my words have caused me deep pain and sorrow. All these years, I did not know how to make amends, for I didn't know where you lived. Now that I obtained your address, I sat down immediately to write you a letter of apology. Please forgive me for having gotten angry at you. Relieve my troubled soul and let me know that you do not bear me any ill will."

Forgiveness — on Condition

Alarge crowd huddled in front of the door of the Gerrer Rebbe's study. Everyone desired the holy blessing of R' Yitzchak Meir Alter, the *Chiddushei HaRim*. R' Bunim the *shammash* had his hands full keeping order among them.

By and large, most people were willing to wait their turn without making a fuss. There was one troublemaker, however, who refused to listen to R' Bunim. He demanded the right to enter next, even though there were many people who had been there ahead of him. When the *shammash* tried to prevent his forced entrance, the man gave R' Bunim a ringing slap.

R' Bunim was shocked and confused. He entered the Rebbe's room and told him what had just happened without mentioning names and then returned to his post.

The people entered the study one by one, in turn, to pour out their hearts and receive the Rebbe's holy blessing. The man who had slapped the *shammash* waited his turn, like the rest, and was finally allowed in.

The Rebbe knew at once that he was the culprit. He refused to hear his plea and rebuked him for his churlish behavior. The man felt ashamed of himself. His eyes filled with tears. "I came to beg you to pray for me, Rebbe. I am childless," he said.

"I refuse to listen to you until you apologize to R' Bunim and receive his pardon. If he forgives you, I will listen to your request."

The man left the room and sought out the *shammash*. R' Bunim had a tender heart and a kind disposition. He could not remain angry at a person who wronged him and would always forgive that person at once.

The man reentered the Rebbe's study together with the *shammash*. "Rebbe," said the *shammash*, "I am prepared to forgive this Jew, but only on one condition."

"And what is that?" asked the Rebbe.

"On condition that the Rebbe bless him with children."

The Rebbe was pleased with this reply. He nodded and blessed the supplicant. Sure enough, within the year, the *tzaddik*'s blessing was fulfilled.

5 Tishrei

On this day, the Romans imprisoned R' Akiva for teaching Torah in public (*Shulchan Aruch: Orach Chaim 560*). He died a martyr's death on the ninth of *Tishrei, erev Yom Kippur*.

"You Are Fortunate, R' Akiva"

R' Akiva lived at the end of the period of the second *Beis Hamikdash* and the years following. He was considered one of the great Sages in his time. R' Akiva was born in 3760 (1 C.E.) and died *al kiddush Hashem*, as a martyr, at the age of one hundred and twenty, in the year 3880 (120).

R' Akiva defied the Roman law forbidding Jews to study

Torah. Despite the grave risk, he would gather huge assemblies and teach Torah to multitudes.

When Pappus ben Yehudah saw this, he asked, "R' Akiva, are you not afraid of the Romans, who have forbidden the study of Torah?"

"I am surprised at you, Pappus," said R' Akiva. "They call you wise, but your question shows that this is not so."

Pappus did not understand what R' Akiva meant. But before he could ask, R' Akiva explained: "Let me give you a parable.

"A fox was once strolling along a river bank when he saw fish swimming frantically this way and that. 'Why are you so terrified?' asked the fox. 'We are trying to evade the fishermen's nets,' explained the fish. 'Well then,' said the wily fox, 'I have excellent advice for you. Come up on land and we will live together.' The fish laughed bitterly at the fox. 'They say that you are the most clever of beasts. How could you give us such foolish counsel? If we are endangered in the water, which is our element, our source of life, how much more so must we fear to go up on land, where we are sure to die!'

"Do you understand my point?" asked R' Akiva. "If our lives are in danger while we study Torah, which is our life and the length of our days, how much more should we fear to cease studying it!"

Despite the evil decree, and in face of the grave danger, R' Akiva continued to study and to teach Torah until the Romans caught him, cast him into prison, and sentenced him to death.

When the time came for him to be executed, R' Akiva began reciting the *Shema*. The Romans dragged him out and lacerated his flesh with iron combs. R' Akiva suffered the torturous pain with resignation. He concentrated all of his thoughts upon the words of the *Shema*, accepting *Hashem's* majesty with love.

His disciples stood by and watched him suffer. They could not contain themselves and burst out, "Rebbe! Enough! How can you focus your thoughts on the *Shema* when you are being tormented!"

He replied, "All my life I have regretted being unable to fulfill the verse 'to love *Hashem* with all your soul,' which means even if He takes away your soul. I wondered if the opportunity would ever arise for me to fulfill the commandment of loving *Hashem* to the point of surrendering my soul? I yearned to fulfill it. And now, that I have been granted that chance, shall I not do so willingly?"

He uttered the words of the *Shema* with painstaking clarity, extending the *'echad'* until his soul expired.

And when his soul departed, a Heavenly voice was heard, "Fortunate are you, R' Akiva, for having died with *'echad'* on your lips. Rejoice, R' Akiva, for you have been granted everlasting life in *Olam Haba*" (*Berachos 61b*).

Hand-Washing in Prison

R' Akiva remained in prison until his execution. R' Yehoshua Hagarsi was chosen to attend him. He came to visit him each morning, bearing a basket of food and a pitcher of water.

One morning, a guard stopped him. "What do you have there?" he asked gruffly. "I must inspect the contents of your basket."

R' Yehoshua stood still and let the guard examine the basket. He peered into the pitcher and asked, "Why must you bring so much water? Your rabbi cannot possibly drink all that water! You must be planning to soften the ground and dig a tunnel under the prison wall. Well, I caught you in time."

He seized the jug and poured out half the water. He then returned it to R' Yehoshua and allowed him to enter R' Akiva's cell.

The guard's inspection and shouts had taken a long time. The aged R' Akiva was weak and hungry. "Why are you so late?" he asked. "You know that it is difficult for me to go without food."

R' Yehoshua explained what had happened. "The guard was so suspicious that he poured out half the water. What a heartless fellow!"

"So be it," said R' Akiva with a sigh. "Come here with the pitcher and let me wash my hands before eating."

"But, Rebbe, you need that water for drinking. If you wash your hands, there will be nothing left."

"What can I do? Our Sages have taught that we must wash our hands before eating. I would rather starve to death than eat without washing!"

When the guards saw that R' Akiva was determined to use the little water for hand-washing rather than for drinking, they permitted R' Yehoshua to fill the pitcher to its brim (*Eruvin 21b*).

This is the sixth of the Ten Days of Penitence. R' Aryeh Leib, the Sabba of Shpoli, passed away on this day. The Sabba, or Zeide, was a disciple of the Baal Shem Tov and considered one of the foremost figures of Chasidus. He was born in Russia in 5486 (1726) and died in Shpoli in 5572 (1811).

Mission in Prison

As was the custom of many *tzaddikim* of former times, the Shpoli Zeide went on a self-imposed exile, wandering from city to city, from town to town.

He once journeyed to a remote village. The Shpoli Zeide had heard that the Jewish innkeeper there was outstanding in his hospitality, and wished to see it for himself. He arrived at the inn and was greeted warmly. Shortly thereafter, another guest, a poor man, appeared, and he, too, was invited to remain over *Shabbos*.

That *Shabbos* was especially uplifting for both the host and his two guests. The two strangers agreed to continue on their way together when they left the inn on the morrow.

While proceeding on their way, the Shpoli Zeide noticed that his companion kept looking back from time to time, as if searching for someone who followed in their tracks.

Soon a wagon appeared behind them on the horizon. When

the poor man saw it approach, he turned to the Shpoli Zeide, saying, "I must go into the forest for a moment. Will you please watch my pack until I return?"

The Shpoli Zeide agreed. He sat down by the road to wait. The wagon approached rapidly and stopped in front of him. The Jewish innkeeper leaped out and was followed by the local village authority, a gross, unruly gentile.

Before the Shpoli Zeide could say as much as a word of greeting, the innkeeper shouted excitedly, "Here is the thief!" They pounced upon him and searched his things.

The Shpoli Zeide did not understand what was going on. Bewildered, he stood and watched. Suddenly, the innkeeper cried out, "I found it! Here are the stolen articles!" He drew out a golden goblet and two silver spoons from the poor man's pack. The man had stolen them from his host, but they were convinced that the Shpoli Zeide was the thief.

They dragged him to their wagon, beating him all the way, and quickly drove to Poltova, which was not far away.

The Shpoli Zeide lay at the bottom of the wagon, almost senseless. They had not allowed him to say a word in self-defense. He was terrified, at first, but then he calmed down and attempted to clear his name once more. His captors sealed their ears against his pleas.

When the wagon reached Poltova, he was handed over to the police. Without any inquiry, he was thrown into jail together with thieves and murderers.

The gentle Shpoli Zeide suffered untold torture in that cell. The criminals persecuted him in every way possible and even demanded that he pay "membership dues."

"But I am no criminal. I didn't do anything wrong!" protested the Shpoli Zeide. "I am here by mistake. I am really innocent."

They laughed in his face and held a trial to judge him for not paying up his dues. The mock judges passed sentence: The

stubborn prisoner was to be punished with a sound flogging. They threw the Shpoli Zeide down to the ground; one man sat on his legs and another on his head while a third was to beat him.

The man had raised his hand and was about to let the whip fall upon his victim when he gave a sudden cry. His hand was swollen to twice its normal size and he writhed in pain.

The prisoners crowded about him, forgetting the execution of the sentence. They wanted to help him, but there was nothing they could do. They shouted for the warden, who took the suffering man to the hospital.

The remaining criminals realized that the Shpoli Zeide had something to do with it. They knew, now, that he was a holy man and were in deep awe of him. From then on, they treated him with the utmost respect and fear.

During the many days that the Shpoli Zeide remained in prison, he came to ask why Heaven had cast him together with these evil men.

He studied the ways of the other prisoners. One of them struck him as a Jew, even though the others referred to him as 'the Gypsy.' He was dark complexioned, but the Shpoli Zeide was certain that he had guessed correctly.

He chose to become friendly with the man and in a short time won his confidence. Slowly, the 'Gypsy' opened up his heart to the Shpoli Zeide and began telling him his life's story.

"I became orphaned of both parents in early childhood. The community supported me until I turned thirteen, but then told me that I would have to earn a livelihood. I hired myself out to a wagoner and soon became an expert on horses, but I earned a mere pittance. I decided to become a horse trader.

"This work brought me in contact with many Gypsies, who were also horse traders. I learned to recognize them and even joined them on their travels. I became very close to them and soon was like a Gypsy, myself.

"Many of these Gypsies were thieves. I, too, became a thief. I was once caught with a stolen horse and was taken to court. The judge sentenced me to a two-year term.

"I have been here already a full year and have one more to go."

The Shpoli Zeide's heart went out to this wayward Jewish soul who had fallen to the depths of depravity. It now became clear to him why he had been sent here: It was his mission to save this soul from doom.

He drew closer to this Jewish 'Gypsy' over the coming days. He learned that his given name was Yaakov. Gradually, the Shpoli Zeide spoke to him about leaving his shiftless ways and returning to his people and his faith.

The *tzaddik*'s words found their way into Yaakov's heart. He showed an interest in the ways of Judaism. He learned how to put on *tefillin* and soon the basic prayers fell fluently from his lips. He also stopped eating *treife* food.

Before long, he was a changed man, a sincere penitent. He prayed to *Hashem* from a broken heart that his *teshuvah* be accepted.

"How will I know if Heaven has forgiven me for my sins?" he once asked the Shpoli Zeide.

"*Hashem* will give you a clear sign, Yaakov, never fear. When the time comes, you will know that your past is erased."

Time passed and that sign materialized. Yaakov learned that his gentile wife and the two children he had had by her had died in an accident. He understood this to be the sign that his past was forgiven and forgotten and that he could start his life anew.

One night, the Shpoli Zeide had a dream. Eliyahu Hanavi appeared to him and said, "Arise and leave this prison. Do not fear. All is well."

The Shpoli Zeide awoke to find himself in his prison cell, as usual. How was he to escape? he wondered. Trusting in

Hashem, he gathered up his few possessions and was about to try the iron door when he suddenly remembered his friend, Yaakov. He could not leave him alone in a den of criminals! Who knows if he would not revert to his evil ways and all the Shpoli Zeide's efforts would have been in vain!

"I will take him along!" he decided. "If *Hashem* performs a miracle for me and helps me escape this cell, He will surely save Yaakov as well!"

He crept over to the 'Gypsy' and woke him up. "Shhh!" he warned him, first. "Get up, quickly, take your things and follow me."

Yaakov followed the *tzaddik* unquestioningly. They reached the door to the cell and found it open. They slipped past the sleeping guards and continued down the corridor. One by one, the doors opened before them until they found themselves at the front gate. Here, too, the guards were sound asleep, as if drugged. The key was in the door. The Shpoli Zeide turned it. The door swung open. They were out, free! They murmured a prayer to the Almighty, the Redeemer of prisoners.

On this day, in 5523 (1762), R' Moshe Sofer, the Chasam Sofer, was born. The Chasam Sofer, a great and brilliant leader, was appointed as rabbi of Pressburg on the seventh of *Cheshvan* 5563 (1802). He established an impressive *yeshivah* in Pressburg which produced hundreds of rabbis who went on to serve Jewish communities throughout Hungary. R' Moshe was summoned to the Heavenly *yeshivah* on the twenty-fifth of *Tishrei* 5600 (1839).

Three Tests Proved His Nature

"*I* have come here to receive *semichah*, rabbinical ordination," said the young man who was shown into the Chasam Sofer's study.

The Chasam Sofer had noticed, with surprise, that he had not kissed the *mezuzah* upon entering, but shrugged it off as an oversight due to his excitement. Just to make sure, he said, "I am sorry, but I have no time to test you today. Please come back tomorrow."

The young man left the room. The Chasam Sofer watched him and saw that he had omitted to kiss the *mezuzah* upon leaving, as well.

The next day, when the young man returned, he, again, failed to put his hand up to the *mezuzah*.

Rabbi Moshe Sofer, the author of the "Chasam Sofer"

The Chasam Sofer turned to him, saying, "You passed through my doorway three times without once kissing the *mezuzah*. Therefore, you are not fit to be a rabbi in Israel. I am sorry, but under no circumstances can I give you *semichah*."

The Rejected Student

Two young students once came to the Chasam Sofer asking to be admitted to his *yeshivah*.

The Chasam Sofer accepted one and rejected the other. The youth who had not been accepted implored him to change his mind, but the Chasam Sofer was adamant; he could not enter the Pressburg *yeshivah*.

The reason for that young man's rejection came to light some time later. From his window, the Chasam Sofer had seen the two approach. A heap of palm branches, which had served just a few days before as the roof for the Chasam Sofer's *succah*, lay on the ground. One youth had trampled upon the branches and walked to the front door, without a care for another's possessions. It was he whom the Chasam Sofer had rejected.

In Whose Name?

The Chasam Sofer was once told that some of his students had repeated what he had said in his Torah discourses in their own name, without giving him due credit.

The Chasam Sofer smiled and said, "Never mind! As long as they don't attribute to my name that which they themselves have originated!"

Rabbi of Pressburg

The distinguished R' Meshulam Igra served as the rabbi of Pressburg before the Chasam Sofer.

After the death of R' Meir Berabi, the *av beis din* of Pressburg, the community wished to appoint R' Yitzchak Charif, the rabbi of Sambur, as his successor. They sent him a letter requesting him to come to Pressburg. Not knowing his exact address, they sent the letter to the head of the community of Sambur and asked him to forward it to the rabbi.

The communal leader, who knew what the letter was about, decided not to deliver it to R' Yitzchak. He certainly did not want to be the instrument causing their beloved rabbi to leave!

The Jews of Pressburg waited in vain for a reply. When several weeks had passed and no answer was forthcoming, they decided to send a second letter. Again, they sent it to the same address and, again, the man ignored it.

The community of Pressburg waited for an answer. Since they did not receive one, they concluded that R' Yitzchak was not interested in their offer.

They then turned to R' Meshulam, rabbi of Tisminitz. R' Meshulam had already decided to leave Tisminitz. Their offer came at an opportune time and he was willing to accept.

However, the Pressburg communal leaders mentioned that they had already approached R' Yitzchak Charif of Sambur, but had received no reply. R' Meshulam decided that before giving a definite yes, he would first go to R' Yitzchak and make sure that he was not interested in the position.

When the community of Sambur heard that the eminent R' Meshulam Igra was coming, they all went out to greet him. R'

Meshulam was invited to stay in the rabbi's house and a banquet was prepared there in his honor. During the meal, R' Meshulam explained the reason for his visit. "Are you certain that you are not interested in serving as rabbi of Pressburg?" he asked.

R' Yitzchak looked puzzled. "But they never offered me that position!"

The head of the Sambur community overheard this exchange. He turned white. He knew that he was the culprit who had tampered with the two letters. At that very moment, those two letters were burning a hole in his pocket, so to speak. He took them out and, with trembling fingers, handed them to R' Yitzchak. The rabbi of Sambur read them and all became clear.

"In that case, I withdraw my candidacy from the rabbinate of Pressburg," said R' Meshulam. "That prestigious office is yours."

"Not at all," replied R' Yitzchak. "It rightfully belongs to you. See, Heaven has contrived events for you to become the next rabbi of Pressburg."

R' Meshulam was duly appointed to that high office. Passing through Pressburg once, the Chasam Sofer stopped by to pay his respects to its spiritual head. The two great men found much to discuss. When the Chasam Sofer rose to leave, his host, R' Meshulam, escorted him all the way to the front gate, a sure sign of his deep esteem for the Chasam Sofer, for he never did so with other visitors.

After R' Moshe left, someone asked R' Meshulam why he had shown such deference to this guest. He replied, "He will one day do Pressburg proud."

Many years passed. On the eighteenth of *Tishrei* of 5562 (1801), R' Meshulam passed away. Pressburg was shattered by the news and could not bring itself to find a successor.

The heads of the community suggested several of the great

leaders of the times, but each time, something stood in the way. Then, some remembered what their own rabbi had said many years before concerning the Chasam Sofer. "He must have wished R' Moshe Sofer to be his successor," they said.

All the heads of the community were in agreement. But, since there had been many suggestions, they decided to take all the names which had been mentioned and cast lots. The rabbi whose lot would be drawn would be appointed. R' Moshe Sofer's lot was drawn. It was clear to all that Heaven had spoken through R' Meshulam.

Without delay, the Chasam Sofer was informed of the results and came to serve as their rabbi.

8 Tishrei

The first *Beis Hamikdash* was dedicated on this day by Shlomo Hamelech in Jerusalem in the year 2936 (824 B.C.E.).

The Foundations and the Water

When King David excavated to lay the foundations of the *Beis Hamikdash*, he dug to a depth of five hundred cubits.

He then descended to inspect the digging and found an earthenware shard. As he stretched forth his hand to pick it up, the fragment spoke to him. "You must not move me for I plug up the waters of the underground Abyss."

But King David decided, nevertheless, to pick up the shard. He moved it only slightly, when the underground waters began surging up, up, up, threatening to flood the entire world.

The king grew alarmed and turned to his counselors, "Tell me what to do! How can we stop this flood?" he asked.

One of his advisers was Achisofel. "The time has come for me to rule over Israel," he thought. "I will wait until the waters drown King David. Then I will halt their rise, since I know the secret. The people, in gratitude, will then crown me king."

Achisofel incorrectly interpreted his prophecy as a sign that he would reign, when, actually, it was his granddaughter who would married a king. This is why he wanted David to die.

The waters rose alarmingly high.

King David turned to his advisers again and said, "If there is anyone among you who knows how to stem the flow and is withholding his knowledge, he shall die by strangulation."

Achisofel was frightened and revealed what he knew: "Your Majesty must write down the Ineffable Name of *Hashem* upon a piece of earthenware and cast it into the water. This will plug up the subterranean vaults of water."

The king did so at once and lo! The waters receded deep into the bowels of the earth until it seemed that the world would be sucked altogether dry!

King David then recited the fifteen chapters of *Shir Hamaalos* (the Song of the Ascents). With each chapter, the waters rose a bit until, after the fifteenth, they reached the safe and satisfactory level (*Succah 53b; Yalkut Shimoni, Tehillim 120*).

This is *erev Yom Kippur*, the day when one seeks out his acquaintances and asks them for forgiveness (*Shulchan Aruch; Orach Chaim 60b*).

The Insulting Butcher

A butcher once insulted Abba Aricha, better known as Rav. He did not apologize at the time, nor did he later ask for forgiveness.

Erev Yom Kippur arrived and he still had not approached Rav. Rav thought to himself, "I know that in my heart, I forgive him. But that does not clear him from blame. If he does not ask my pardon, he will bear his sin and be punished for it, and I don't want that to happen. I will go to him. Surely, when he sees me, he will remember that he insulted me and will ask me to forgive him. Then his sin will be erased and forgotten."

Rav, one of the most prominent Sages of his generation, cast aside his honor and went to the butcher. He passed by the store, hoping that the butcher would see him and step out to apologize, but he did not. Rav walked to and fro, trying to draw the butcher's attention.

The butcher was chopping bones.

He looked up and saw Rav. "Go away," he said rudely. "You have no business here."

The moment he said that, a small fragment of the bone he was chopping flew up. It pierced his throat and he fell dead to the ground.

Forgiven!

R' Yosef Dov Soloveitchik, rabbi of Brisk, was sitting in the *beis medrash* studying with his brilliant son, R' Chaim.

A butcher burst in and, at the top of his voice, hurled abuses and curses at R' Yosef Dov. The previous day he had been involved in a *din Torah* before R' Yosef Dov. When the ruling had gone against him, he had concluded that the rabbi had accepted a bribe and ruled in favor of his opponent. "The rabbi has taken a bribe," he declared. He grew so violent that he threatened to strike the rabbi.

R' Yosef Dov and his son sat in silence. After he had expended all his energy, the butcher left the *beis medrash*. R' Yosef Ber rose from his seat and walked after him. "I forgive you!" he said. "I forgive you!"

On the following day, the butcher went to the market to buy cattle for slaughter. As he was inspecting the animals on sale, a bull attacked and killed him.

R' Yosef Dov heard about this and was shaken. "It is my fault," he berated himself. "Perhaps he was punished because of my resentment. Oh, to think that I am guilty of having killed a fellow Jew!"

"But you did forgive him, Father!" said R' Chaim comfortingly. "You must not blame yourself."

R' Yosef Dov was not to be consoled. "How can I be sure that I really forgave him from the depths of my heart?"

"But I heard you say so," his son assured him and even pointed to the spot where his father had stood when he had said, "I forgive you."

R' Yosef Dov relaxed somewhat, but the pain would not go away. When the butcher was buried, he went to the funeral and followed the bier all the way to the grave, weeping bitterly. He did not rest until he had undertaken to recite *Kaddish* and study *mishnayos* for the sake of the butcher's soul throughout the entire year of mourning. Nor did he stop at that. Each year, on the anniversary of the butcher's death, he would fast, for he feared that he had been to blame for his death, because he had not fully forgiven him.

A Conditional Pardon

When R' Yosef Dov Soloveitchik traveled, he would remove his rabbinical garb and put on simple clothing; he would exchange his rabbinical hat for an ordinary cap with a visor.

Thus attired, he once reached Benowitz. It was a stormy, bitter-cold night when he knocked on the door of the Jewish inn at the crossroads.

The door opened. "I have no room for you," grumbled a scowling innkeeper. "I am expecting guests tonight and have no place to spare." He was about to slam the door on the shivering traveler and leave him to fend for himself, when R' Yosef Dov pleaded, "All I want is a roof over my head until morning. I don't even need a bed. But, please, don't turn me out on such a night. I might freeze to death!"

Only after much coaxing and pleading did the innkeeper, finally, admit the traveler. He led him to a corner in the hallway and said, "You can lie down here. That's all I can offer." And with that, he went into one of the clean, heated rooms in the inn.

R' Yosef Dov had no intention of sleeping. He took a candle from his pocket and began to study by its light.

A moment later, a door was flung open and the innkeeper poked his head into the hall. "Put that candle out at once!" he shouted. "You are disturbing everyone's sleep!"

R' Yosef Dov blew out the candle and continued to study by heart. He soon forgot his cold and discomfort in the heat of his study.

Hours passed and then the rumble of wheels was heard on the nearby road. Several wagons rolled up to the inn. The expected guests had arrived.

The innkeeper ran to open the door. He greeted his guests warmly; they were R' Aharon of Koidenov and a group of his chasidim.

After they had shed their coats and warmed themselves at the hearths in their rooms, the Rebbe prepared to say the evening prayers. He went out to wash his hands and happened across the figure huddled in the hallway.

One look and he drew back in alarm, "Is that you, R' Yosef Ber? What is the rabbi of Brisk doing here on the floor?"

At the sound of his shocked voice, the innkeeper hurried out. When he learned the identity of the figure in his dark, cold hallway, he was seized by trembling. He lowered his head in shame, remembering how disgracefully he had treated this great man.

When he had recovered somewhat from the shock, he approached R' Yosef Dov, knees knocking, and wept, "Please forgive me, Rebbe. I didn't know who you were."

"I forgive you," the rabbi reassured him, "but only on one condition."

"Yes! Anything you say," said the innkeeper hastily.

"The condition is that you come to Brisk and be my guest for two weeks."

"Very well," said the innkeeper.

The innkeeper traveled to Brisk and was welcomed into the rabbi's home. There he learned the meaning of hospitality. He saw how one should greet and treat guests. He saw how R' Yosef Dov personally tended to the needs of his community, individually and collectively. He saw how R' Yosef Dov treated the poor, how he comforted the downtrodden and helped whomever he could.

At the end of the two weeks, he had learned a great deal. He returned to his inn a different man and became an example of fine hospitality. Soon, he had earned a reputation as a generous host and a man of unstinting charity.

The Postponed Pardon

A man once came to R' Eliyahu Lopian and said, "I did something terrible to you and I have come to ask your forgiveness."

"If you like, I can say the standard 'Machul lach — you are forgiven'," said R' Eliyahu Lopian. "But since you say that you committed something terrible, I am afraid that that will not suffice. I might not forgive you with my whole heart. But I have a suggestion — come back in two weeks."

"And what good will that do?" asked the man.

"During those two weeks, I will increase my study of mussar (ethics) on the subject of forgiveness and the evil of bearing a grudge and harboring ill will. I hope that by the time

HaGaon R' Eliyahu Lopian feeding a cat

you return, I will be able to forgive you, and mean it with my whole heart."

When the man returned two weeks later, he was greeted by R' Eliyahu who said, "Now I feel that I can forgive you, heart and soul."

Yom Kippur.

Confusing to Whom?

*T*he heads of the community of Mezibuz, the seat of the Baal Shem Tov, once sought to abolish the accepted custom of placing plates on a table in the synagogue into which people threw coins for various charities. "The clinking of the coins causes noise and confusion," they maintained.

When the Baal Shem Tov heard of this, he objected vehemently. "The sound of the coins also confuses our adversaries in Heaven," he said.

How to Cry

*E*ach year on *erev Yom Kippur*, R' David Moshe of Tchortkov would weep. Whoever was fortunate to see him weeping was struck by his intense fear and awe of the Day of Atonement, and the onlooker, too, would experience great awe.

Once, his son, R' Yisrael, entered his room. Seeing his father shedding copious tears, he became petrified with holy dread and could not move a finger.

His father saw him thus and said, "Do you see, my son? This is how one must weep when he does not behave as he should."

"The King . . ."

When R' Aharon of Karlin reached the section in the morning prayers of the Days of Awe that begins with "*Hamelech* — the King," he fainted and was only revived with great effort.

"What happened? Why did the Rebbe faint?" asked the chasidim. He explained that when he had reached the word "*hamelech*," he was suddenly reminded of a story in the *gemara*.

Rabban Yochanan ben Zakkai lived during the difficult siege of Jerusalem and saw the people dying from hunger. He succeeded in leaving the city and appeared before the Roman commander Vespasian. "Peace unto you, O emperor," he greeted him. Vespasian was astonished. "You deserve to be put to death," he said. "If you consider me emperor, why did you not come until now?"

R' Aharon turned to the chasidim and said, "If that is true with regard to a mortal king, how much more so with the King of kings! How much more so should we show our recognition of the King of kings! Small wonder that I was overcome when I reached the title 'the King' and fainted!"

Laboring Before Hashem

The *shammash* of R' Dov Ber of Lubavitch left the Rebbe's room on *Yom Kippur* bearing the Rebbe's long coat. The chasidim noticed that he carried it by his fingertips, since the garment was soaked through, as though it had been fished out of the water. The *shammash* was taking care to avoid squeezing out any of the perspiration and, Heaven forbid, overstepping a Torah prohibition on *Yom Kippur*, itself.

As he passed near the chasidim, he murmured, "See how the Rebbe exerts himself for your sake?"

The Rebbe was forced to change one coat after another on the Holy Day, so greatly did he perspire from his mighty efforts. For the Rebbe prayed with his whole body, from the depths of his heart and soul.

On this day, Moshe Rabbenu began to judge the Israelites by Torah law and to teach it to them. This took place in year 2449 after the Creation (1311 B.C.E.) *(Shemos 18:13, see Rashi there)*.

The Laws of Hashem Are Righteous

*M*oshe Rabbenu was shown the future to the end of all generations. He saw the evil and corruption that mankind would be heir to and the hatred that man would harbor towards his fellow man.

Moshe was appalled and saddened by the fate of the innocent, the poor, the oppressed and the robbed ones. He turned to *Hashem* and asked, "Judge of the earth, why is there injustice? Why does the *tzaddik* suffer and the evil one prosper? Why do You overlook all the evil that takes place in the world? I beseech You, explain Your ways. Tell me how You mete out justice so that I might understand it. For I know that Your ways are true and good. Tell me, that I might tell others of Your righteousness."

Hashem replied, "Since you have implored Me to explain how justice prevails, I will show you an example. But I cannot show you everything, for you are only flesh and blood and incapable of understanding or accepting everything I could show you."

Moshe opened his eyes and saw:

A mounted soldier approached a small stream of clear, bubbling water, dismounted and let his horse drink its fill. He then knelt by the water to quench his own thirst. A heavy pouch of money fell out of the folds of his garment, but he did not notice. Having slaked his thirst, he mounted his horse and continued on his way.

Soon a young shepherd came by, leading his flock to water. The youth saw the pouch and, picking it up, realized that it contained money. He joyfully stuffed it into a fold of his garment and thought, "Now I will not have to continue working for my harsh master who thrashes me mercilessly. I can stay home and help my widowed mother. I shall buy her a house and a field and support her comfortably to the end of her days. Thank you, *Hashem*, for Your great bounty!"

An old man came to the stream. He had been walking for a long time and was dusty and tired. He slumped down at the water's edge, panting. After a few moments, he opened his pack and took out a few dry crusts which he dipped in the water before eating. After eating and drinking, he lay back to rest, pillowing his head with his small bundle of belongings. Soon he was fast asleep.

Meanwhile, the soldier discovered the loss of his money. "I must have dropped it when I bent over to take a drink," he thought. He turned the horse about and rode back to the spot where he had stopped to drink.

Searching about for his money pouch, he came upon the old man fast asleep. "He must have found my money!" he thought. He ran over and shook him awake. "Where is the pouch? Give me back my money!" he demanded.

"What money?" murmured the old man sleepily, not understanding.

"My money! The pouch you found here! It fell from my robe and you must have found it and taken it."

"I? A pouch full of money? I don't know what you are talking about! I stopped here to have a drink and then lay down to sleep. I found no money."

The soldier refused to believe him. "But no one else was here. You must have taken it and are lying. If you don't give me back my money at once, I will kill you."

The old man took no heed of the threat. He knew that he hadn't taken the money. He gathered up his few belongings and was about to walk away. His silence enraged the soldier, who was certain that he had taken the money. In a fit of anger, he fell upon the old man and killed him.

He searched thoroughly through the old man's belongings and saw that the money was truly not there. But it was too late. Disappointed, he continued on his way.

When Moshe Rabbenu had seen these events, he said to *Hashem*, "Almighty G-d, how pained I am by what I have just seen. An innocent old man was murdered by an evil man who went unpunished. And a poor little boy became rich in the short span of a moment! How am I to understand all this?"

"Lift your eyes, Moshe, and see the ladder before you. Climb it until you reach a rung which no mortal has ever reached. There you will behold how righteous My acts are."

Moshe ascended the ladder until he reached a high rung. From there he was able to see the following:

A farmer was limping along, a little boy at his side. Suddenly, an old man approached him and, without any warming, leapt upon him, killed him and stole his money. A soldier was standing nearby, witness to the crime, but he did not lift a finger to help the man under attack.

"Now that you have seen this," said *Hashem*, "I will explain everything. The old man who was murdered at the water's edge was the same old man who murdered the crippled farmer and stole his money. The soldier who killed the old man is the very soldier who stood by and did not come to the farmer's aid.

"The old man who killed the farmer fled with his money, but the pouch fell out of his pocket and the soldier found it. It did not belong to him, however, and so, he lost it. The young shepherd who found it is that farmer's son and thus, the money is rightfully his!

"So you see, Moshe, that, ultimately, all of My ways are just. The old man who committed murder was himself murdered. The soldier who did not come to the rescue of the murdered man slew the murderer. And the money which was stolen from the farmer was retrieved by his orphaned son, as it should be."

"Indeed," said Moshe, "*Hashem* is, truly, a righteous G-d, without iniquity. He is just and upright."

Three days before *Succos*.

A Doubly Dear Mitzvah

R' Moshe of Lelov was very old when he decided to leave his birthplace, Poland, and settle in *Eretz Yisrael*.

The Rebbe acted swiftly after his decision. He took leave of his thousands of chasidim and admirers and set out together with his sons, grandsons and the rest of his household.

The journey by sea was lengthy and hazardous in those days. Unfit vessels were buffeted by the waves for many months before they reached their destination. R' Moshe's ship was to be at sea for many months, including the month of *Tishrei*.

R' Moshe was prepared. He had a *shofar*, the *arba'ah minim (lulav and esrog)* and even timber to set up a *succah* on deck.

The *shofar* and the timber needed no special care. But R' Moshe was concerned that the *lulav* and *esrog* remain fresh.

A few days before *Succos*, when R' Moshe inspected them again, he saw, to his dismay, that while the *esrog, lulav* and *hadassim* were in good condition, the *aravos* (willows) had withered; they were unfit for use.

The *tzaddik* was woebegone. But, although he did not have *aravos*, as of the moment, he refused to forgo the *mitzvah* of *arba'ah minim*.

R' Moshe approached the captain with a suggestion: Instead of continuing on as scheduled, would he sail for the nearest port so that R' Moshe could obtain fresh twigs of willow for *Succos*?

The captain burst into laughter at this ridiculous request. Did this elderly Jew really expect him to change his course just to satisfy a foolish whim? It was unthinkable!

His mocking laughter did not deter R' Moshe. He offered the captain a large sum to make him change his mind.

"Nothing doing!" said the captain stubbornly. "I won't change course just for a few miserable twigs."

R' Moshe was not put off. He raised his offer higher and higher until he had reached the sum equal to all the money he had brought along, the savings from which he expected to live to the end of his days in Jerusalem.

When the captain heard the amount he was suggesting, he agreed to dock at a nearby island. Willows grew there and soon, the Rebbe had what he required — the fresh *aravos* for his *lulav*.

With indescribable joy, he bound them together with the *hadassim*. He had spent a fortune — all he possessed — for the *mitzvah*. Should he then, not rejoice doubly, as if he had found a great treasure?

R' Akiva Eiger, rabbi of Posen in Prussia, passed away on this day. He is one of the most famous Jewish leaders of all time. He was born on *rosh chodesh Cheshvan* 5520 (1759) and died in 5598 (1837).

Honor for Whom?

*T*he Jews of Nikolsburg were gripped by excitement: R' Akiva Eiger was traveling on his way to Eisenstadt in Hungary to celebrate his daughter's marriage to the famous Chasam Sofer. He was stopping in Nikolsburg to pay his respects to R' Mordechai Banet.

The whole community, young and old, turned out to greet the famous man. All longed to catch a glimpse of his holy face. The city's scholars even had the privilege of exchanging Torah thoughts with the brilliant man.

What an honor! The Jewish community of Nikolsburg was beside itself with joy for there were few people who could compare in stature with R' Akiva Eiger.

While everyone was impressed by the guest, R' Mordechai was very reserved in his judgment. He had spoken with him and R' Akiva Eiger had not uttered even one *chiddush*! "Why do people make such a fuss over him?" he wondered. "I spoke to him and found nothing exceptional."

R' Akiva remained in Nikolsburg for a few days before traveling on. But he soon returned to Nikolsburg to discuss an important communal matter concerning a small village which had problems needing urgent attention.

This time, R' Akiva did impress R' Mordechai with his brilliance and aroused his deep respect. He invited the visitor to speak to the congregation on the approaching *Shabbos*.

R' Akiva agreed. That *Shabbos* he ascended the *bimah* and began to speak.

R' Mordechai Banet, who was present, began to argue and even contradict the guest during the course of the speech. R' Akiva did not defend his position. Instead, he stopped in mid-speech, left the platform and returned to his place.

After the prayers, the guest returned to his lodgings. R' Mordechai thought about how he had interrupted the eminent speaker and had deep misgivings. "Did I insult him? Did I hurt his feelings?" he asked himself. His conscience bothered him and he decided to visit R' Akiva at his lodgings and ask his forgiveness.

When he spoke to him, he saw that R' Akiva was not hurt or embarrassed in the least. Now, in the privacy of his room, R' Akiva defended his position and gently showed that R' Mordechai had been mistaken in his challenge.

R' Mordechai listened and had to concede to his learned guest. He apologized for having interrupted him. "But why didn't you defend yourself in the synagogue?" he asked.

"You are the rabbi of this city," replied R' Akiva modestly, "and the rabbi of the entire country. You deserve your community's undivided respect. I felt it to be poor taste and bad etiquette to contradict you in public, for I am only a passing visitor, here today and gone tomorrow. There is no need for them to give me respect and honor, while you must command their esteem at all times."

R' Mordechai, in his righteousness, was determined to set

HaGaon R' Akiva Eiger

the record straight. He summoned the entire community to the synagogue and told them what had happened. "I learned two important things," he said. "First, I was given an insight into the greatness of R' Akiva in Torah, but even more, I saw the extent of his holiness and righteousness. Upon his first visit to Nikolsburg, he concealed his greatness and succeeded in fooling me. Now I see that not only is he a brilliant scholar but also a person of rare humility."

Who Will Write the Letter?

"**W**hen the Prussian government passed a law abolishing Jewish elementary schools, the *chadarim*, R' Akiva Eiger, rabbi of Posen, convened an assembly of rabbis from all the corners of the land. It was decided to send the king a letter requesting that he rescind the law.

The next step was to find someone expert in German to write the crucial letter. The name of a certain Jew from Posen was brought up. "His German is impeccable and his style excellent," said the one who suggested him.

To everyone's surprise, R' Akiva Eiger disapproved of the proposal. "The man is far removed from Jewish practice; he rejects his Jewish tradition. He is probably well satisfied with the new law. How, then, can we expect him to put his heart into the letter asking that it be abolished? The verse, 'Place your trust not with the magnanimous ones, with a man who cannot help' (*Tehillim 146*), refers precisely to a man like him. He cannot possibly be expected to bring the salvation, if his heart is not in the request. Even if his letter sounded pleasing and convincing to our ear, it could not be relied on to be effective, for he thinks differently from what he writes. No, he cannot be relied on to help us!'"

Erev Succos.

"With Righteousness Shall I Gaze Upon Your Face"

R' Chaim of Sanz devoted his entire lifetime to charity and kindness. While his own family suffered want and hunger, he only had eyes and ears for the distress of others. Much money passed through his hands and all of it was distributed among the poor and needy; he left nothing for himself and his family.

R' Chaim had a tradition from the Ari that on *erev Succos* one should be especially generous. He would give all the funds he had on hand to anyone who approached him on the fourteenth of *Tishrei* and would even go to great lengths to borrow more. Beyond that, at times he would pawn his household possessions and distribute every penny he received to the poor.

One year, on *erev Succos*, to everyone's surprise, R' Chaim was not involved in his usual practice. They found him sitting by his table, sighing deeply. Why was he not distributing charity right and left, as usual?

"He must be feeling ill," said the members of his family, and asked about the sighing.

The *tzaddik* shook his head. He felt well. "Go and fetch the wealthy chasidim who are staying in the inns of Sanz," he told his family.

Soon the wealthy visitors stood before R' Chaim. He turned to them saying, "*Rosh Hashanah* has already passed; *Yom Kippur* is behind us. And I have not yet repented! How can I dare show my face in the *succah*?'

He fell silent. The chasidim were shaken and shocked. Their shoulders slumped helplessly and they wondered, "If the Rebbe has not yet repented, where do we stand? Surely at the very bottom of the ladder!"

"I need several thousand coins for charity, but I have no money. If you agree to lend me that large sum, I will be able to repent properly and within a few weeks, I will return the money to you, please G-d."

Without hesitation, they drew out their purses and laid the full sum upon the Rebbe's table. R' Chaim's eyes lit up and his face was suffused with the joy he usually felt on the Festival.

Night fell. The prayers were over and R' Chaim of Sanz walked home, towards the *succah* in his courtyard. He paused for a few moments in front of its entrance. Facing the head of the table, he said, "*Rosh Hashanah* has passed; *Yom Kippur* is behind us and I have not yet repented! How do I have the audacity to step into the *succah*? Ah, but there is hope. 'With righteousness (charity) shall I gaze upon Your face; I shall sate myself upon Your image while awake.' Only in the merit of the charity I distributed today do I presume to enter the *succah* to gaze upon *Hashem's* glory."

Jewish men selecting the choicest arba'ah minim in honor of Succos

R' Chaim's Succah Decoration

One *erev Succos*, R' Chaim told his sons that he urgently needed two thousand rubles. This was an enormous sum, but his sons went and approached the rich people of Sanz and were soon able to present the entire sum to their father.

The money was hardly in his hands before it had disappeared! R' Chaim distributed it among the needy who constantly besieged him.

That evening, when he entered the *succah*, which was neither luxurious nor fancy, he looked about him and said, "People are accustomed to decorate their *succah* with the finest of ornaments and precious things, but not I. My decorations are the *mitzvos* I bring along into the *succah*, the charity which I distributed today. This is the true glory and grandeur that enhances a *succah*."

This is the first day of *Succos*. On this day in 5656 (1895), R' Mordechai of Nadvorna passed away. He was born in 5584 (1824) and headed the illustrious Nadvorna dynasty.

For a Tree Is like unto Man

*T*he city of Nadvorna was struck hard by a virulent epidemic. In order to prevent its spreading further, the authorities passed stringent sanitary regulations.

With the approach of *Succos*, R' Mordechai of Nadvorna set to work erecting a *succah* in his courtyard, as he did each year. As he was working, a city official appeared with an order to demolish the structure, since R' Mordechai had no permit and it was a violation of the health code.

The Rebbe, with the Torah's ordinances before his eyes, disregarded the warning. When the city magistrate learned of his defiance, he sent another messenger demanding that the booth be torn down at once.

"I erected this *succah* to stand, not to be demolished," declared the Rebbe.

When the magistrate heard this, he sent the rabbi a summons to appear before him, but R' Mordechai ignored this as well.

The magistrate came to the rabbi and warned him in person. "I command you to tear down this structure immediately!" he said forcefully. "If you persist in disobeying, you will be severely punished."

These strong words made no impression upon the rabbi. "I built this booth to stand," R' Mordechai repeated coolly, "not to be demolished."

The magistrate fumed, but before he could open his mouth, R' Mordechai continued, "Let me tell you, sir, that R' Meir of Premiszlan was my granduncle."

"What do I care about your granduncle!" shouted the man in a rage. "I demand that you remove this health hazard, and that is final!"

"Know that R' Meir of Premiszlan was my granduncle. If you have the patience, I will tell you an admirable story."

The magistrate saw that he had no choice and settled back to listen to the story.

"There was once a clergyman with ten sons, all tall and stalwart young men, strong as cedars. This priest had a lovely orchard surrounding his house; its trees were a delight to behold and its fruits were a treat to the palate.

"One day, he decided to chop down part of the orchard and plant flowers in its stead. He uprooted a number of trees, and laid out plots for colorful flowers.

"But as soon as the flowers began blooming, his sons took ill. At first, the oldest one took to his bed. He pined away, until he breathed his last. The second one fell ill and wasted away, until he, too, died. The third, fourth and all except the last died in a similar fashion. Upon the death of the ninth, the youngest also fell ill.

"The priest was beside himself with grief. Now that he was about to lose his last son, he was distraught. He called in the best doctors to treat his son and even consulted fortunetellers, but no one could help the lad.

" 'Since you have nothing to lose, you might as well travel to the Jewish saint, R' Meir of Premiszlan,' suggested a friend. 'He is said to perform miracles and save the lives of the hopeless.'

"In the throes of despair, he rose and traveled to Premiszlan. There he poured out his stricken heart before the rabbi. 'Of my beautiful family, all I have left is one son, and it seems as if he does not have much longer on this earth,' wept the priest. 'Only a miracle can help him now.'

"The *tzaddik* listened sympathetically and said, 'You had a magnificent orchard — did you not? — with luxuriant trees. But you were not satisfied with their luscious fruit and tantalizing fragrance. You desired a flower garden and chopped down your wonderful trees. But know, sir, that a tree is a living thing. A tree is like a man; you cannot sever its life willfully without paying a price. You chopped down the trees of *Hashem* and *Hashem* chopped down your trees, your sons. But now that you have come here, I assure you that your youngest son will live. I will pray for his recovery and his salvation is near.'

"My granduncle, the saintly R' Meir of Premiszlan, prayed for that son, for he wished to sanctify the name of G-d in this world, and the youngest son recovered.

"You are that tenth son and your life was spared, due to the prayer of a holy Jew. Is this the way you show your gratitude, by ordering my harmless booth to be torn down? Surely, my granduncle, R' Meir, deserves more than that for thanks!"

Shivers ran up and down the magistrate's spine. "You are right," he said humbly. "It is true that I am alive only thanks to R' Meir. Forgive me. You may keep your booth and even erect ten more like it, if you wish."

R' Mordechai only needed his one *succah*. And it stood firm and erect for the duration of the Festival. No one disturbed it.

The second day of *Succos*.

The Orphan and the Esrog

R'Shlomo of Radomsk would tell his chasidim the following tale:

The *esrog* dealers joined together one year and formed a cartel to raise the prices. The cost of one *esrog* was so exorbitant that the leaders of one community did not even have enough money to buy one for the entire congregation. (In those days, because of their high prices and the difficulty of obtaining the *arba'ah minim*, it was generally impossible for each person to have his own private set.)

The Festival was approaching and still they could not afford a single *esrog*. The *gabbaim* called a meeting of the rich householders and asked each to donate a sizable sum so that, together, they would be able to purchase at least one *esrog* to complete a full set.

At the meeting, one wealthy man rose and said, "In my humble opinion, it is highway robbery to let the dealers get away with this. We must not submit to them. If we don't have enough money to purchase an *esrog*, we will simply have to do without. We all know the popular saying, 'What does a community do if it lacks an *esrog*? It does not make the blessing.' Don't you think that it is far more commendable to spend such a sum on marrying off the poor orphan girl in our midst?"

R' Shlomo explained, "The orphan in question was getting on in years. But in all those years, interestingly, that rich man had not thought that she should be married off. But when the question of buying the *esrog* arose, his evil inclination showed up and argued that marrying off a bride is a more important *mitzvah*.

"And that," concluded the Rebbe, "is human nature. Often, when a person is about to fulfill a certain commandment, along comes his evil impulse and asks, 'Why did you choose this particular commandment over all others?' And he suggests a different *mitzvah* which, he claims, is worthier than the first.

"One must expose this wile of the evil inclination for what it really is. Then one can fight it and fulfill the *mitzvah* which he has set out to do."

On the evening of this day, the eve of the eighteenth of *Tishrei*, R' Nachman of Breslov, the great-grandson of the Baal Shem Tov, passed away. He was born in *Nissan* of 5530 (1770) and founded the Breslov Chasidus which has tens of thousands of followers to this very day. R' Nachman died in 5571 (1810).

The Emperor and the Rebbe

Napoleon Bonaparte was determined to conquer the world. The French emperor's troops captured land after land to fulfill their ruler's desire to impose French rule and French culture upon all of Europe and the mid-East.

Napoleon reached Egypt and swept it by storm. His next step was to conquer the Holy Land.

While Napoleon's forces were marching towards *Eretz Yisrael*, the young R' Nachman of Breslov was in Tsefas, immersed in the holy study of Kabbalah, according to the teachings of the Ari.

R' Nachman often secluded himself in the ancient cemetery of Tsefas where so many great sages were buried. There, he found himself able to soar spiritually and reach great heights in his service to *Hashem*.

One evening, when he was all alone in the cemetery, he fell

into a deep slumber. An old man in white garments appeared to him and said, "Stop your prayers and hurry to T'veryah on the Kinneret, where you will be charged with a vital mission."

He awoke and remembered the dream distinctly. Without delay, he gathered up his belongings and went to T'veryah.

He rented a small room on the banks of the great lake and continued to immerse himself in Kabbalah, prayer and deep introspection.

Napoleon's soldiers were then encamped on the shores of the Kinneret. Shortly before, the French had suffered a defeat near Egypt at the hands of British admiral Lord Nelson.

Meanwhile, France itself was in a turmoil, on the brink of civil war. Small wonder that the army's morale was at a low point. The soldiers sought to vent their frustration upon the villages near their encampment. From time to time, they would break into the homes of the inhabitants, rob them and oppress them in various other ways.

Once, they attacked the house in which R' Nachman was staying. The landlord was a poor, worthy old man, who recited *Tehillim* all day and was supported by his fishermen sons.

"Give us all your money," they demanded.

"I am a poor man. I have nothing here," said the frightened old man.

The soldiers refused to believe him. They ransacked the house, certain that valuables were hidden somewhere. But they did not find a thing.

Angry and disappointed, they seized the old man and beat him. "Where are you hiding your money, old one!" they shouted at him, pummeling him roughly. "Where are your treasures?"

"I have nothing," he insisted. "Leave me be." His pleas only increased their anger and they lashed out at him in fury.

The old man's cries reached R' Nachman who sat in his

room. He rushed out and, seeing the band of soldiers, shouted indignantly, "Leave him alone! Immediately!"

Murder burned in the eyes of the hardened French soldiers, but they were struck with wonder at the young man who, unarmed and single handed, had the courage to stand up to them and dispense orders.

Then, one of them turned to him with a sneer and said, "Do you want a taste of the same medicine? Come here, we'll be glad to oblige."

Their leader leapt forward and was about to seize R' Nachman, but the moment he looked into R' Nachman's blazing eyes, he froze on the spot, unable to move hand or foot. Two others rushed to his aid, but they, too, became rooted to the spot.

"Give all your money to this old fisherman as compensation for mistreating him!" he ordered.

The three were suddenly able to move again. They thrust their hands into their pockets and emptied them out before the old man. But he was still so frightened that his shaking fingers could not even gather up the coins.

"Lay the old man to rest in his bed," ordered R' Nachman. "Gently!" Without a word of protest, they lifted him carefully and laid him on his bed.

"And now, begone with you. And woe if you dare disturb the peace of the inhabitants again."

Wordlessly, the soldiers turned to go. They disappeared quietly from the scene.

The story of the courageous young man — who had single-handedly, and without weapons of any sort, subdued a large group of armed soldiers — spread throughout the area. The tale reached the French barracks and became the topic of the day. The soldiers who had been the villains of the tale did not deny it, but vividly described what had happened. Soon, even Napoleon heard of it.

Napoleon did not relish what he heard; that a simple Jew had put his soldiers to shame. He ordered a thorough investigation of the matter. "And I want the findings reported to me personally!" he demanded.

Napoleon was skeptical about the matter, but the soldiers who had witnessed the scene first-hand had been deeply impressed. And from then on, they and their fellow soldiers feared to approach the Jewish homes in and around T'veryah.

Thus, one day, when the Jews saw a French officer accompanied by two soldiers approaching their houses, they were surprised. The three made their way through the streets until they arrived at the door of the fisherman's cottage where R' Nachman lived. The two privates were afraid to enter, but the officer was under orders to investigate the matter and had no choice but to go in.

In a corner of the room stood a rickety bed upon which lay an old man moaning in pain. A young man stood at his side, nursing him tenderly. The officer assumed that this must be the wondrous Jew who had stood up to the soldiers and subdued them. "Are you the man who defied the French soldiers?" he asked.

"I only told them to stop beating an innocent old man."

"Who are you to tell French soldiers what to do?" said the officer angrily.

"I saw no justification for their cruelty towards an innocent person. They had no right barging into a private home, wishing to rob an old man of his possessions and beating him mercilessly," replied R' Nachman indignantly.

The officer could not help being impressed by R' Nachman's self-confidence and firmness. Clearly, this was a noble character, an admirable person. He drew him into conversation and soon the subject turned to Napoleon's campaign and his chances for victory. The French officer was amazed to hear brilliant, well-informed ideas flowing from the Jew's lips. R'

Nachman was versed in politics and military tactics and even suggested solutions to difficult problems that had disturbed Napoleon in the course of his wars.

Upon his return to camp, the officer gave a glowing report about the young Jew; his admiration was apparent to Napoleon.

Now, R' Nachman often sought solitude in the midst of nature. On moonlit nights he would sit by the shores of the Kinneret and study. He was so absorbed, once, that he failed to notice a rowboat skimming towards the shore until it was upon him and its occupants had leapt out and made their way towards him.

R' Nachman rose to his feet and bowed towards one of them, "Greetings, Your Majesty!" he said.

It was Napoleon, himself. The emperor was deeply moved. "How did you know who I was?" he asked in amazement.

"The Torah endows wisdom on those who study it," R' Nachman said simply.

Napoleon engaged him in conversation and soon reluctantly admitted that his officer had not exaggerated in praising this young man. He truly was unusual. He was a man of keen perception and understanding.

Duly impressed, Napoleon turned to R' Nachman for advice. "Do you think it worthwhile for me to continue my campaign towards Asia and attempt to conquer the entire world? Or should I return to France and solve its internal problems?"

R' Nachman wrinkled his brow in thought, then replied, "I see that a great future awaits you, but not in the realm of world conquest. You are best off returning to France and using your talents for the good of your people. Know that the road to success entered upon in blood will also end in blood. Wars and battles do not lead to peace but engender additional war and bloodshed. Furthermore, it is important to remember that

people do not make history; rather, Divine Providence shapes its course."

Napoleon had never heard anyone speak this way and was deeply impressed. However, his craving for glory on the field of battle was insatiable and it tipped the balance. He said to R' Nachman, "I prefer a short but glorious life with dazzling military victories over a long life of monotonous, staid peace."

"So be it," said R' Nachman. "To each his own. Nevertheless, you must not forget, Your Majesty, that the heart of kings and ministers are in the hand of the Creator."

Firm in his resolve, Napoleon took leave of the rabbi, but before going, raised one last issue, "Would you be willing to join my staff of advisers?" he asked.

"I, too, have chosen my way in life," answered R' Nachman, "though mine does not lead to fame and glory. All I strive for in life is to serve my Creator with all my heart and soul."

R' Nachman wished the emperor well and each pursued the path he had adopted.

Napoleon soared with dizzying speed to the pinnacle of fame. He became the greatest man alive. But his meteoric rise reached its apex very quickly. Then, his star faded. He spent the remainder of his life a prisoner in exile.

R' Nachman's life was also short. At a young age, he was summoned to the Heavenly Academy, having reached spiritual heights rarely ascended by others. He was acclaimed the leader of thousands of chasidim, who revere his memory and follow his teachings to this very day. His grave in Uman draws Jews from all over the world.

The Ox and the Sheep Laughed

R' Nachman of Breslov used to convey his elevated thoughts to his disciples through stories and parables.

One gem in the treasury of "R' Nachman's Stories" tells about a wicked king who decreed that whoever did not accept the religion of the land would be banished and his property would become the possession of the state.

When the Jews who lived in the land learned of the new decree, they employed every possible effort to abolish it. But they failed. And so, they prepared to leave that land, for their faith was dearer to them than anything else.

They packed their few possessions, took up their staffs and left the land where they and their ancestors had lived for many years.

A small handful of very wealthy Jews could not bear to be parted from their property and chose to accept the state religion outwardly. They hoped to keep up their Jewish practices secretly. One such Jew held a distinguished position in the royal court.

Shortly after the decree went into effect, the king died and his son succeeded him. Despite his youth, he ruled with an iron fist. Craving power and riches, he embarked upon many wars and looted the captured lands. Headstrong and stubborn, he refused to heed the counsel of his wise and elderly advisers.

These elderly advisers felt insulted by the new king's disregard and they decided to overthrow him. "We will kill the king and his family and then we will rule," they said.

When the secretly Jewish counselor heard of the plot, he

revealed it to the king. "He is a wicked king and headstrong and thoughtless," he said to himself, "but better that the kingdom remain in his hands than dissolve into anarchy." He also had a selfish reason for doing so. If the government fell into the hands of the conspirators, there would be widespread riots and looting and he would suffer. Above all, he wished to protect his wealth.

He approached the king and told him about the plot against him. The king appointed new bodyguards to protect the palace day and night and was always on the alert for the sign of an uprising.

When the plotters struck, he was ready. He quickly seized them and threw them into prison. They were tried, convicted of treason, and sentenced to severe punishment.

The king was not ungrateful. He summoned his loyal adviser and said, "You saved my life and the lives of my family. How can I repay you? What reward do you ask? I swear that your wish will be my command."

He thought for a moment, then said, "Your Majesty, I do not ask for honor, riches or power. Nevertheless, I do have one request."

"What is it?"

"I am a Jew. Your father's decree forced me to forswear my religion. I continued to practice it secretly while professing to embrace the religion of the kingdom. I lead a double life. I beg of you, Your Majesty, to allow me to live openly as a Jew."

The king hated himself for having made such a rash promise to his adviser before having heard what it was that he wished. For this king was no different than his father; he hated Jews. But having promised, he agreed to allow the loyal minister to return to his religion, while waiting for the first opportunity to withdraw this permission.

The king never carried out his secret wish, for he died shortly thereafter and his son succeeded to the throne. The young king took note that both his father and grandfather had died young. "I want to live a long, full life!" he declared. He gathered all of his counselors together and asked them how he could best assure himself of long life.

Their first piece of advice was that he reinforce the law forbidding Jews from living in the land. "Jews are a spreading poison. Once you are free of them, you will reign for many years!" they said unanimously. All of them were determined to oust the Jewish minister from his favored position.

The king decided to follow their advice. He summoned the Jewish adviser and said, "I am not bound by my father's oath. I, therefore, give you the choice of leaving our country or converting to the national religion. If you leave, your property will become the possession of the state."

The Jew tried his best to change the king's mind, but in vain. The new king was adamant. Again, the Jew failed to stand up to the test; he could not bear to part with his money and power and again, outwardly converted.

That night, the king had a strange dream. He found himself looking toward heaven at the twelve constellations. To his consternation, two of them, the ox and the lamb, were laughing at him!

When he awoke, he was puzzled and alarmed. His uneasiness did not leave him. He summoned all of his wise men and astrologers and asked them to interpret his curious dream.

"The answer is very simple, Your Majesty," they said. "The ox and the lamb will bring about your premature death," predicted the stargazers.

When the king heard this, his heart pounded with fear.

"Is there any way to avert the evil?" he asked hopefully.

"There is. Slaughter all of the oxen and sheep in the land. When there are no oxen and sheep, the dream will be meaningless."

The king did not delay but issued a proclamation that within the week, all the citizens were to slaughter their flocks. Whoever disobeyed the royal decree and was found with a live lamb or ox would be severely punished.

The populace hastened to carry out the king's decree, fearing his heavy hand. Within days, none of those animals could be seen in the land and the king felt safe once more.

When the danger no longer hovered about him, the king decided to go out to war, as had his father and grandfather. At first, he scored victory after victory and his pride swelled accordingly. He was so assured of winning that in one campaign he took his family along that they should, with their own eyes, bear witness to his great might. But he was defeated and he and his family were slain on the battlefield.

When the people of the kingdom heard the terrible news, they appointed a new king, to prevent anarchy. The new king assembled his wise men and astrologers and asked them, "How can it be that the former king and his entire family were wiped out in such brutal fashion if he followed your advice?"

Not knowing what to reply, they lowered their heads in shame.

Then, one of the advisers arose. It was the secret Jew. "I have an answer, Your Majesty," he said. "Your advisers deceived you, Sire. They misinterpreted the dream and led the king astray."

Before anyone could disagree, he continued, "As you know, I am a Jew. We had a great king in ancient times named David. He waged wars to defend his people and succeeded even in defending them from a fearsome giant, Goliath. But this was not the essence of his greatness. King David's greatness lay in his ability to compose holy psalms in praise of his Creator. He wrote these beautiful psalms with Divine inspiration and prophecy. And in his book, the Book of Psalms

(*Tehillim*), King David correctly interpreted our former king's dream. His interpretation is altogether different from that of advisers and stargazers."

"Indeed?" said the king, his curiosity aroused. "Tell me, then, what is the true meaning of that strange dream?"

"Among our many commandments are two very important ones: that of *tefillin*, phylacteries, and that of *tzitzis*, ritual fringes. The leather boxes of the *tefillin*, the *batim*, are made from the leather of cattle, that is, oxen, while the fringes are made from sheep's wool. The ox and lamb, which mocked the king when he looked up at the constellations, symbolized the two commandments which are incumbent upon all male Jews. They laughed because he tried to do away with the commandments by expelling the Jews and driving their practices from his land.

"This is what King David referred to when he said, 'Let us sever our reins' — the straps of the *tefillin* — 'and cast off our ropes' — the thickly entwined strings of the *tzitzis*. But, as the verse goes on to say, 'The Dweller in Heaven laughs.' The Almighty mocks those evil rulers who try to sever the Jews from their commandments.

"If only those evil monarchs knew how much benefit Jews bring to their lands by living in their midst and obeying the commandments of their faith, they would implore them to keep the laws more strictly, with greater zeal and fervor ..."

These words appealed to the new king. He immediately abolished the decrees of his predecessors and issued an invitation for all Jews from foreign lands to come and settle in his country.

This is the fourth day of *Succos*. On the evening of this day in 5574 (1813), R' Yaakov Yitzchak of Pshischa, the Yehudi (Yid) Hakadosh, passed away. He was born in Pshedburz, Poland in 5526 (1766) to R' Asher, the rabbi and *maggid* of the town. R' Yaakov Yitzchak was one of the early founders of Chasidus and teacher of many great Polish-Jewish leaders.

The Quiet Transformation

*I*t was a frosty winter night. A thick carpet of snow had already blanketed the ground and mighty winds shrieked in bloodcurdling sounds as they blew the steadily falling snowflakes every which way. People huddled around their hearths or snuggled under cozy quilts. No one thought of venturing out in this hostile storm.

Midnight. Soft footsteps could be heard in one of the houses. R' Asher, candle held high, crept up to his little son's bed and thought fondly of the sleeping figure. "Perhaps he is cold and needs another blanket." He reached the bed and froze in panic.

It was empty. The child was gone!

"He must be wandering about the house," thought the father hopefully, his heart pounding. He searched through the rooms, but little Yaakov Yitzchak, aged seven, was nowhere to be found. He had vanished!

His wife awoke to the sound of the footsteps. She could not believe that Yaakov Yitzchak was not in bed. "But I, myself, saw him saying the *Shema* before going to sleep! Where can he be?" she cried frantically.

The anxious parents decided to leave their warm house and search the snow-covered streets. On the far side of the front door, they saw small footprints in the fresh snow.

"Look! He went out!" they cried simultaneously, and followed the tracks which led them to the synagogue. The interior was lit by a single candle. And by the light of that candle their little boy was pouring out his heart in prayer before his Creator.

Oblivious to the biting cold, the happy parents stood by a window transfixed, listening avidly. His voice penetrated deep within them. Pleasure and joy now took the place of fear. "How sweet his voice is! How beautiful is his prayer!" exclaimed the mother.

Little Yaakov Yitzchak stood alone in the large synagogue. The single candle threw a dancing light upon the walls and upon his *Tehillim*, as the psalms fell lovingly from his lips. Yaakov Yitzchak repeated phrases over and over, explaining them anew. He stood imploring, beseeching, an errant son before his Father.

They listened carefully to his words and became doubly glad. The boy was begging of *Hashem* that He open up his heart to understand Torah, that his heart might cling to the *mitzvos*, that he be steadfast in his love and fear of *Hashem*.

The parents stood in the cold, their ears pricked up to catch every precious syllable. Time passed. They were thickly coated by the falling snow; the wind whipped mercilessly at their exposed faces, but the parents were blissfully happy and unaware of any discomfort. Their eyes were glued to the figure of their dear son praying so ecstatically; they could not budge from the spot.

Finally, finally, they returned home, frozen and soaked to the marrow. They could not sleep that night. They waited eagerly for their son, wondering what he would do and say.

Shortly before dawn, they heard his light footsteps crunching on the frosty snow. Yaakov Yitzchak opened the door quietly and slipped into bed. He pretended to be asleep.

A bare half hour passed. He leaped out of bed, alert and eager to begin the new day. Strong as a lion, fresh, bursting with vigor, he showed no signs of having remained awake the entire night.

The day ended. The parents quietly kept track of their son's actions. At midnight, they heard Yaakov Yitzchak rise from his bed with hardly a rustle, slip into his clothing and leave the house.

The moment he disappeared into the darkness, his father rose and tiptoed after him. This night, as on the previous night, the footsteps led directly to the *beis knesses*.

His father watched as he poured his heart into the moving words of the psalms. He said each verse and explained it in many different ways, which were deep in meaning and aroused feelings of *teshuvah*. R' Asher stood spell bound by the window, listening to his son's outpouring. When he finally returned home, his son was still in the midst of his heartfelt prayers, unaware that he had been watched.

The following night and all the nights afterwards were the same. At midnight, Yaakov Yitzchak would arise and leave the house. His father would follow behind and, watching from the window, would glow with pride at the beautiful interpretations that fell from his son's holy lips.

R' Asher addressed the community every *Shabbos* on the weekly portion. But from the night that he discovered his son praying in the synagogue and illuminating the verses of

Tehillim with different, marvelous interpretations, he changed the subject of his sermons. He would devote his talks not to the weekly portion, but to a chapter of *Tehillim*, and explain the verses as he had heard his son interpret them. When he was asked the source of these marvelous explanations, he would smile but would not reveal their origin.

His audience was always enthralled with these speeches. His words fell like balm upon their souls. They drank them thirstily and craved for more. Small wonder that people talked about them and wondered where the rabbi derived them from.

His audience grew from week to week, until the synagogue could barely contain everyone. They were enchanted by the beautiful meanings which the words of the familiar psalms suddenly took on.

One week, the synagogue could no longer contain the crowd and some had to stand outside by the windows to catch the precious words of his sermon.

The women's gallery was also packed with women and children, for the rabbi's words found a way into their hearts, too. These were words of the living Torah, life-giving waters.

R' Moshe Leib of Sassov, the great defender and protector of Israel, lived at this time. He was accustomed to travel about and visit the different communities to see how his people were faring. He sought to comfort the downtrodden and help the suffering wherever he could, for his magnanimous heart overflowed with love for the Jew. He regularly visisted Pshedburz, where R' Asher served as rabbi every few months.

He arrived once and headed for the synagogue, which was always his first stop before going on to the markets and streets. He wished to feel the pulse of the people and mingle among them, from the scholars to the tradesmen and the beggars.

There was something different about the town, this time, intangible but felt. He found that the attendance at the daily classes in Torah study had increased. Wherever he went, the synagogues were full. He studied the people's manner of prayer and noticed that it was less automatic, more sincere and fervent. Most marked of all was the change in the market-place. Gone were the shouts, curses and foul language that had always typified it; absent were the abuses and occasional blows exchanged by the coarse peasants and dealers. Every-thing was toned down, quiet and sedate, pleasant and serene. The stalls were filled with produce and people bought and sold in modulated tones, dealing fairly, the haggling reduced to a courteous murmur.

The town had taken on a different sheen. A new peacefulness had settled down upon Pshedburz. "What was responsible for it?" wondered R' Moshe Leib. Who had brought this change about?

He inquired, but no one could answer his question. The people themselves were hardly aware of the transformation that had taken place and could not tell him what had caused it.

R' Moshe Leib was overwhelmed. He was determined to get to the bottom of the mystery. He delved and dug until he was able to put his finger on the crux of the phenomenon. It had all begun with R' Asher's *Shabbos* lectures on *Tehillim*, which had become so popular that the entire town attended them. Not only that, they had affected people's behavior and the entire demeanor of the town had changed for the better.

When R' Moshe Leib heard this, he decided to remain over *Shabbos* to hear a sermon with his own ears.

Shabbos came and R' Moshe Leib was one of the huge crowd which came to hear R' Asher speak. R' Moshe Leib listened thirstily, and immediately sensed that the words emanated directly from a pure and holy source.

Shaken and excited, he listened to every word. Afterwards, he approached R' Asher and asked to speak to him privately.

When they were alone, R' Moshe Leib asked, "Tell me, where did you find those beautiful explanations?"

At first, R' Asher tried to evade the question, but R' Moshe Leib pressed him and finally ordered him to reveal the source of his speeches. R' Asher could not disobey the *tzaddik* and disclosed his secret. "I hear these stirring concepts from my seven-year-old son, Yaakov Yitzchak, each night," he said. "I remember them and deliver them on *Shabbos*."

The mystery was out. R' Moshe Leib examined the young child and discovered that he possessed an exalted and holy soul. He grew close to Yaakov Yitzchak and, whenever he visited Pshedburz, would spend time with the child, conveying some of his own Divine spirit to the blessed boy.

They say that R' Moshe Leib of Sassov was one of the first *tzaddikim* to acknowledge the boy's greatness and the measure of his future impact upon his people. He drew him near to Chasidus and schooled him to become the master and teacher of his people, the leader hailed as "the Yehudi Hakadosh."

This is the fifth day of *Succos*. On this day in 5558 (1797), R' Eliyahu, the Gaon of Vilna, passed away. The Gaon was born on the fifteenth of *Nissan* in 5480 (1720).

No Need for a Doctor

R' Eliyahu, the Gaon of Vilna, usually spent the entire week isolated in his room alone, enveloped in his *tallis* and wearing *tefillin*, studying Torah. He spoke only what was absolutely necessary, even to his own family, disciples and close acquaintances.

On *Succos* he was a different person. He would be blissfully happy, sitting in his *succah*, surrounded by his circle of followers. He spoke freely with them, asking after everyone's health and affairs. But, even when he emerged from his isolation during this period, he devoted hours upon hours to Torah.

Once, when he was seated in his *succah*, deeply engrossed in a difficult subject, a young man of his close circle entered, thinking that the Gaon would not mind company. But R' Eliyahu was so involved in his study that he was unaware of the intrusion. He did not look up or utter any greeting.

The young man remained for some time. Seeing that he was

The Vilna Gaon — R' Eliyahu of Vilna

being ignored, he left, feeling hurt. "Perhaps the master is angry with me," he thought sadly. "He is always happy to see me on *Succos* and always asks about me and my family. There must be a reason why he did not even glance my way."

The young man sought out a friend who was also a close

disciple of the Gaon and poured out his heart to him. "Rabbenu must be dissatisfied with me for some reason, for he did not even greet me when I entered his *succah*," he said sadly.

"That cannot be!" said his friend. "He must have been so engrossed in study that he did not even notice you come in."

The young man refused to be comforted. He continued to be morose and disturbed.

Seeing him thus, his friend said, "Do you know what? Let's both enter the *succah* together and see what happens. I will ask the Gaon directly if he is at all angry at you."

The two went to R' Eliyahu's *succah*. The second young man asked, "With the master's permission, I would like to know if you bear any rancor against my friend, here."

"G-d forbid!" replied the *tzaddik* at once. "What makes you think that? May he live to be a hundred!"

That young man reached extreme old age, he was hale and hearty, never having suffered any debilitating illness or physical ailment.

When he was ninety-eight, he became ill. Deeply concerned, his family wished to summon a doctor to his bedside, but he restrained them. "I still have two years of life. I am sure that I will not lose even one day of the blessing that the Vilna Gaon gave me, never fear!"

This is the sixth day of *Succos*.

Which One Is the Fool?

After fleeing with his family from Spain, the Rambam lived for a while in Fez, Morocco.

One *Succos*, after prayers, he left the synagogue, holding his set of *arba'ah minim* in his hand, for, the *gemara* tells us, this was the practice of worthy men living in Jerusalem.

The king of Morocco happened to pass by, just then, and, seeing this unfamiliar sight, summoned him and said, "Tell me, what this is all about? Why are you walking about waving palm branches in the air like a crazy fool?"

"Your Majesty," said the Rambam. "This is not silliness on my part. Fools throw stones, whereas this is the custom of the wise men of Jerusalem and of our Jewish forebears many generations ago." The Rambam was alluding to the Moslem custom of throwing stones upon arriving in Mecca, the holy Moslem city.

The king did not catch the Rambam's meaning, but his ministers did. They were furious at the clever, quick-witted reply and its hidden barb.

"Your Majesty," they said, turning to the king, "the Jewish physician is mocking our holy customs." They explained the Rambam's comment to the king.

The king became equally incensed. "Seize him at once!" he shouted. "Put him to death!"

But the Rambam was out of reach, by now. His father, R' Maimon, had been told that R' Moshe's life was in danger and the family had fled from Fez to a safe haven.

21 Tishrei

Hoshana Rabbah.

The Snuffbox

On *Rosh Hashanah*, a chasid in the Baal Shem Tov's *beis medrash* dropped his snuffbox in the middle of the service. He quickly bent down to retrieve it, and, before putting it back into his pocket, took a pinch and inhaled it with pleasure.

His neighbor wondered at such behavior in the midst of prayers on this holy day. "How unseemly it is to bend down for a snuffbox and take such a hearty pinch of tobacco!" he thought angrily.

The Baal Shem Tov sensed his thoughts and knew that such thoughts would arouse a Heavenly accusation against the owner of the snuffbox.

He wished to spare him evil consequences and tried to defend the chasid in Heaven, but the accusation remained. *Hoshana Rabbah* arrived and during the *maariv* prayers, the Baal Shem Tov was able to arrange for a possible exoneration of the owner of the snuffbox. If his accusing friend would himself find merit for the owner, the man would be excused from punishment. But the Baal Shem Tov was not permitted to reveal this information to either of the chasidim.

When he entered the *beis medrash* at night, the Baal Shem Tov noticed that the chasid who had the critical thoughts was saying the special prayer-arrangement for *Hoshana Rabbah*, the *tikkun*, but something was lacking. The chasid was distracted and seemed unable to concentrate upon the words. He arose and paced back and forth. Foreign, disturbing thoughts flew into his head. "Why was tobacco discovered in this last generation as a stimulant to be smoked and inhaled?" he found himself thinking. "It must be," he answered his own question, "that tobacco is, somehow, beneficial." And, suddenly, he regretted having judged his friend so harshly on *Rosh Hashanah*.

The night passed. The Baal Shem Tov always made himself available to answer his chasidim's questions on *Hoshana Rabbah*. They would prepare their questions beforehand, whether on Torah subjects or other matters.

The critical chasid asked about tobacco. "Is there any benefit in tobacco and snuff?" he said.

"What do you have to say?" prompted the Baal Shem Tov.

The chasid repeated the thought that had struck him the previous night. "That is not the entire story," said the Baal Shem Tov. "Tell it all."

The man unfolded the tale of the snuffbox. "At first, I condemned my friend's crude behavior," he said, "but on second thought, I found some credit in his act and was sorry for having thought ill of him."

"Let me tell you that your censure aroused a serious Heavenly accusation against him," said the Baal Shem Tov. "But that has been canceled now, through your favorable judgment of him. In the future, however, you must be careful to always judge your fellow man in a favorable manner so as to prevent an indictment being made in Heaven."

Shemini Atzeres. We recite a special prayer for rain.

Kalman Prays for Rain

There was a heavy drought. The rainy season had almost passed without a drop of rain. The skies were a bright summer blue; not a wisp of cloud marred their expanse. All the cisterns were empty and the wells had dried up. The town was dying of thirst and disease.

The rabbi of the city decreed Mondays and Thursdays as public fast days and told the wealthy people to distribute large sums to charity. Everyone was called upon to pray for the heavens to release their blessed rain. But nothing changed. The skies remained a summer blue, without a sign of rain.

When he saw that the prayers went unanswered, the rabbi examined his deeds and the deeds of his congregation. Had anyone sinned in such a terrible fashion that Heaven was withholding life-giving rain? He searched and searched, but could find no cause for this terrible punishment.

The suffering of the entire town; the cries of the young and old; the agony of mothers who sat helplessly watching their children die from hunger and disease — all these tore at the rabbi's heart. He secluded himself in his attic and prayed intensely, "Master of the world! Show me what to do to repair our wrongs and save my flock who are wasting away from lack of rain."

It was midnight and the rabbi heard a voice in his dream. "Do not multiply your prayers. They will not be accepted. You will not be answered until Kalman, the storekeeper, leads the congregation in prayer."

The rabbi awoke in a panic. "Could this dream be significant? Why, Kalman, the storekeeper, is an unlearned boor. Not only is he ignorant, but he is always getting into fights with his customers. He is also known to be a tight-fisted miser who shuns the community. Why should he be the one to lead the prayers for rain? What a silly notion! It must have been an inconsequential dream, nothing to be taken seriously."

The rabbi sequestered himself in his attic the next day, too, and prayed with all his might. "Have mercy upon Your creations!" he wept. "Save us for the sake of the innocent children who have never sinned. Send Your sustaining rain to revive our wilting bodies."

That night, the rabbi heard the mysterious voice whispering to him again: "Why waste your breath in prayer and tears? It is all in vain as long as Kalman, the storekeeper, does not lead the community in prayer. Only he can save you."

The rabbi awoke, his heart in a turmoil. "Now I know that it was not a meaningless dream," he said, "for it has repeated itself. I must carry out what the voice said."

As soon as morning dawned, he called an urgent meeting of the communal officials. "Gather all the townspeople to the synagogue for prayer," he said. "Everyone must attend."

"Who will lead the prayers?" they asked.

"I will select the suitable person at the proper time," said the rabbi tersely. He was ashamed to admit that Kalman, the boor of a storekeeper who could barely read, was to lead the prayers.

The synagogue was soon filled from door to door. Even the women's gallery was packed. Everyone was present, from young to old. They had all come to pour forth their prayers to Heaven. And the question almost seemed to slice through the air of the *beis knesses*, "Who would lead the prayers?"

"Kalman, the storekeeper, step up to the *bimah*," announced the rabbi. Kalman always sat by the door at the back of the synagogue.

Kalman? Had they heard correctly? Had the rabbi said, "Kalman"? But the community was full of worthy men, men of deeds and men of learning! Why Kalman, of all people? How could a boor like him represent all the fine Jews assembled here and have his prayer penetrate the Heavenly barriers to bring rain? Who knew if he even understood the words of the prayer?

The rabbi sensed the undercurrent in the synagogue and repeated, "Will Kalman, the storekeeper, please step up to the *bimah*." Kalman himself was surprised, but he left his place at the back of the room where the porters and laborers sat, those who were thought of as simple Jews, and shuffled his way forward. "Reb Kalman," the rabbi turned to him, "please begin."

"Is this some mean joke, Rabbi?" asked Kalman in surprise. "Are you making fun of me? You know that I can barely make out the words in the *siddur* and do not begin to understand them. Why pick on me?"

"Never mind. I asked you to lead the prayers and I insist that you do so. That is the decree of Heaven. As for the words, say what you know and try your best."

The storekeeper did not say a word. He removed his *tallis* and *tefillin* and marched out of the synagogue.

"Let's appoint someone else," suggested the officials hopefully. "After all," one blurted out, "Kalman is only an ignoramus. He is not fit to lead the prayers."

"He is probably off to his shop, so as not to lose any customers," added another snidely.

"No. We shall wait half an hour. If he does not return by then, we will send people out to search for him," said the rabbi adamantly.

The words were hardly out of his mouth when Kalman appeared in the doorway, panting and puffing. In his hand he held a scale. Everyone recognized it; it was the one he used in his store. And with the scale he approached the *bimah*.

Confused whispers flew. "What is he doing?"

"What does he expect to weigh here? His many good deeds? Ha!"

Kalman lifted the scale high above his head. He raised his voice and the people stopped their murmuring. "Master of the world," he declared. The evenly balanced sides of this scale are like the two letters *heh* of Your Name. The rod from which they are suspended is like the *vav* in Your Name. The hook which supports the entire scale is like the *yud* of Your Name.

"Master of the world! If ever I lied, cheated or gave a false weight, if ever I short-changed anyone on this scale and besmirched the letters of Your Name represented here, let fire descend from Heaven and consume me on the spot!

"But, if I never lied or cheated with this scale, if I never tarnished Your Holy Name, then I beseech You, Merciful King, to send us Your blessed rain at once!"

He fell silent. The synagogue grew dark. The windows rattled and a cold wind blew in. Lightning flashed, followed by a peal of thunder. Then came the familiar, but almost forgotten sound — a pitter-patter on the synagogue roof.

"Rain! Rain!" they shouted excitedly. The rabbi wished to speak and point out to the people the importance of accurate weights and measures, but everyone had rushed out to see the miracle, to feel it, to drink their fill after so many weeks of thirsting.

It was later learned that all the tradesmen of the city had had faulty weights — except for Kalman. Therefore, only he was worthy of praying on behalf of his brethren for *Hashem* to tip the scales in their favor and grant the Heavenly blessing of rain.

23 Tishrei

Outside of *Eretz Yisrael*, this day is celebrated as *Simchas Torah*.

Reason to Rejoice

One *Simchas Torah*, R' Menachem Nachum Dov of Sadigura turned to one of his chasidim and said, "We finished reading the Torah today. But why do we start it again on the very same day?"

Before the chasid could venture a reply, the Rebbe said, "There is a good reason. Let us imagine a Jew in the synagogue today seeing the rejoicing and dancing upon the completion of the Torah. Might he not become depressed at the thought that an entire year had passed during which he had hardly studied it? What part could he take in the celebration!

"To prevent him from becoming despondent, we begin the Torah anew, as if to say to him, 'It does not matter that you failed to study until now. Here is your chance to start from the beginning. The gates of Torah are open again to you!' "

R' David Moshe of Tchortkov

Not Difficult Now

R' David Moshe of Tchortkov was a sickly, weak individual. On *Simchas Torah*, he ignored his frailty and whirled around with a Torah scroll in his arms during many *hakafos*. He danced ecstatically and would not give up the precious scroll, even when he was exhausted.

His disciples stood by and watched him with deep concern. The *tzaddik* was not strong, but he was dancing with all his might, holding a heavy burden. Was it not beyond his capacity? "Is this not too strenuous for the Rebbe?" they asked him anxiously.

"Strenuous?" R' David Moshe replied in wonder. "It is only difficult before one takes the *sefer Torah* in one's arms. But once you embrace it, it is no longer difficult."

His chasidim understood the allusion. It was a lesson in life. When a Jew wishes to accept the yoke of Torah, the idea seems staggering. But once a person becomes accustomed to it, it is no longer difficult or burdensome, but a deep joy.

On this day in 5542 (1781), R' Yaakov Yosef Hakohen, rabbi of Polnea, passed away. R' Yaakov Yosef was the Baal Shem Tov's outstanding disciple. His work, *Toldos Yaakov Yosef*, the first to be written by a leader of the chasidim, was printed in 5540 (1780). Many incisive sayings which he heard from his master, the Baal Shem Tov, are to be found there.

The Rejected Book

After *Toldos Yaakov Yosef* was first printed, its author, R' Yaakov Yosef, would travel from place to place to sell it. Its price was one gold coin.

His travels eventually brought him to Berditchov, which was, in those days, full of scholars. He laid copies of his *sefer* on a table in the *beis medrash*, but no one was interested in buying. R' Yaakov Yosef was grieved that the people of Berditchov did not appreciate the great wisdom it contained, the teachings he had heard from his master, the Baal Shem Tov.

The *tzaddik*'s disappointment had repercussions in Heaven and a terrible fire broke out in Berditchov. It raged far and wide, threatening to burn down the entire city.

R' Ze'ev of Zhitomir, who lived in Berditchov at the time, understood that the fire was not caused by natural reasons, but

that it was a sign of Heavenly wrath. He hurried over to R'
Yaakov Yosef and asked, "Why are you so upset that no one
is buying your work? Look, the Almighty also wrote a *'sefer'*
which is surely no worse, Heaven forbid, than yours. He
peddled His Torah, as it were, to all the nations, but not one of
them was prepared to buy it. They all rejected the Torah, for
one reason or another. Was this cause for Him to become
wrathful and destroy the world?"

When R' Yaakov Yosef heard these wise words from R'
Ze'ev, he was appeased. And at that moment, the fire abated
and died out.

25 Tishrei

On this day in 5571 (1810), R' Levi Yitzchak of
Berditchov passed away. A saintly man, he was one
of the great early figures of Chasidus.

The Perfect Comfort

The community of Berditchov numbered a great
many Jews, yet each one considered himself like an
only son of R' Levi Yitzchak. Each one knew that if he
ever became ill, the Rebbe would rush to his side and
care for him like a loving father.

R' Levi Yitzchak once went to visit one of the sick members
of the community. The man was on his deathbed, tossing
about from side to side. He was, clearly, very worried.

"What is troubling you, my friend, at such a time?" asked the *tzaddik*.

"Rebbe," he whispered weakly, "I feel that my hours are numbered and my heart is full of fear. I am standing on the threshold of the World of Truth. I have repented my sins on my deathbed, but with what merits shall I be going to my final judgment? What will my portion be in the World-to-Come?" Tears flowed from his eyes.

R' Levi Yitzchak bent over him and said, "You have no cause for worry. I am hereby giving you my entire portion in *Olam Haba!*" Without hesitating, he gave over to him his most precious possession!

The man lay back, relieved. His face relaxed in a contented smile. And thus, in a spirit of trust, he returned his soul to his Maker.

R' Levi Yitzchak's deed aroused wonder among his followers. After the man died, they asked him, "Rebbe, when you entered the room, you saw that the man had only a short time to live. You could have reassured him with any comforting saying. Why were you so generous as to give him your entire portion in *Olam Haba?*"

The *tzaddik* of Berditchov replied movingly, "I would rather give away my entire reward in the World-to-Come than allow a Jew to suffer a moment of pain and worry!"

On this day in 5587 (1826), R' Asher of Stolin passed away. R' Asher was born in 5520 (1760). A holy figure, he guided his hundreds of chasidim along the path of righteousness.

On Whom to Rely

Year in and year out, hundreds of chasidim would visit Stolin to celebrate *Pesach* with the Rebbe, R' Asher. A chasid, who was accustomed to do so, was told one year that he would be unable to cross a certain river during his journey. The spring thaw had begun and large ice floes swirled dangerously downstream, making passage by rowboat too hazardous. Since the river was no longer frozen over, he could not cross on the ice, either.

He did not turn back, however. He was so eager to spend *Pesach* with his master that he decided to cross, come what may. He was risking his life, he realized, but he began picking his way across the ice, leaping from one floe to the next. He feared that he might fall and drown in the raging waters at any moment. Each step seemed to be his last, but he persevered until, miraculously, he reached the other side.

He sped on to Stolin and rushed into the Rebbe's house. R' Asher was aware of the risk he had taken to get to Stolin and was angry with him. He even refused to give the chasid his

hand in greeting. "Who asked you to endanger your life for my sake?" he rebuked him. "I will someday have to give an accounting for myself of this incident before the Heavenly Throne and explain why I allowed a Jew to risk his life. What shall I say?"

In order to bring his point home, the Rebbe told his chasid a story from the *Midrash*:

In the time of King David, a poor man was walking along the road when he was attacked by a bandit, who threatened to kill him. The poor man pleaded for his life. "What will you gain by killing me?" he asked. "I have no money to give you."

"I am afraid," said the bandit, "that you will go to King David and tell him where you met me. He will then send his soldiers to trap me and bring me to justice."

"But I swear that I will not breathe a word of this encounter to the king. Just release me and let me go my way."

"But King David has Divine intuition. If you ever meet him, he will read upon your face that you were captured by a notorious criminal. He will catch me and kill me, even if you do not utter a word!" The bandit unsheathed his knife and plunged it into the luckless man's heart.

As a result of this murder, King David was asked, "Why did the world have to know that you are endowed with Divine intuition? It brought about a man's death!"

"I, too," concluded the Rebbe, "may be punished because you considered me a holy person and, relying on my merit, risked your life to come to me. You should not have depended on me and expected a miracle. Now, I will be taken to task for it!"

On this day in 5573 (1812), R' Aryeh Leib Hakohen passed away. He enriched our people with his outstanding works which have become basic texts: *Ketzos Hachoshen*, *Avnei Miluim* and *Shev Shematsa*.

Torah Through Suffering

R' Aryeh Leib's early life was beset with poverty and suffering. He was so hard pressed that he lacked the money to buy a table or the materials to construct one himself.

But how could he record his brilliant thoughts if he did not have a table to write on?

He found a solution. A wooden board placed over a barrel served as his writing surface.

He had no money for firewood to fend off the fierce European winters. His stove stood cold and neglected in a corner of the freezing room. R' Aryeh Leib was chilled to his bones and his stiff fingers could not easily even hold a pen, let alone move it across the parchment. But nothing deterred the genius from accomplishing his holy work, not even the most bitter cold. Nothing crushed his indomitable will. Like a courageous lion, he leapt over all obstacles.

R' Aryeh Leib sat in his room and wrote, despite all the

handicaps. Sometimes the ink in his inkwell froze. But he was driven to express the thoughts that gushed forth like a fountain. He would put the inkwell under a pillow to melt the ink. After it thawed, he would continue on — writing, writing, writing.

Three Portions, Three Books

One *Yom Kippur*, R' Aryeh Leib became ill. His condition was such that his life was in danger.

The doctor warned R' Aryeh Leib that if he did not drink and eat, he would surely die.

He was left with no choice but to eat on this holiest of days. This deeply grieved him. He knew that it was the right thing to do, but it pained him greatly, nevertheless.

With a heavy heart, he prepared the minimal portion he would have to eat to stay alive. He divided it up into three parts, each of which was less then the measure forbidden by the Torah to eat on *Yom Kippur*.

Three times during that day, he partook of food. During those moments, his suffering was so terrible as to be unbearable.

But Heaven rewarded him. In return for having been forced to eat three times on *Yom Kippur* and, because of the suffering that accompanied the eating, he was granted the privilege of writing three great scholarly works.

On the evening of this day, R' Avraham David of Butchatch passed away. He was born on the sixth of *Adar*, 5531 (1771) and passed away in 5601 (1840). His works, *Daas Kedoshim* and *Eshel Avraham*, serve as fundamental texts in halachic literature.

A Profitable Trip

Silence reigned in the room where the distinguished scholars of Yas were grappling with a difficult problem. Their lined faces reflected their concern; the atmosphere was oppressive.

Then a voice was heard: "Why are we wasting our time on this complex problem? Why don't we present it to a great man and let him guide us?"

Why hadn't they thought of that before? The group quickly decided to turn to R' Avraham David of Butchatch. They would ask him to come to Yas. He would open their eyes to the truth, for he was known as a saintly man.

The communal leaders quickly chose a delegation of distinguished men to fulfill the important task of asking R' Avraham David to trouble himself to come to Yas.

The men chosen were venerable men of inspiring stature and appearance, but one of the delegates stood out from the rest, being much younger than they.

When the group reached Butchatch, they went at once to the rabbi's house. Trembling with awe and hope, they entered his study and presented the purpose of their visit; they waited anxiously for his decision.

"I will go!" was his gratifying answer.

Their eyes lit up and they breathed a sigh of relief. What a heavy burden had been lifted from their shoulders! Now they could rest assured that their problem would be solved, since it was in such trustworthy, capable hands.

The rabbi called to his *shammash* and told him to prepare provisions for a journey. "I will be gone for several days," he said.

The delegation from Yas was overjoyed to hear that he wished to accompany them without delay. They thanked *Hashem* for their success.

They left the rabbi's study and waited outside. They could not help congratulating themselves on their good fortune. The young chasid was especially exuberant. "I am certain," his voice rang out above the others, "that the Rebbe's trip will not be in vain and that he, too, will benefit. The people of Yas will undoubtedly shower him with gifts of money."

After a moment, the door opened wide. The Rebbe stood there; he did not look as if he were about to leave. "Forget about the preparations for the trip," he called out to his *shammash*. "I am not going."

The announcement hit the delegation like a bolt of lightning.

"Why, Rebbe? What has happened?" they asked in wonder. They stood there, confused and shocked, not knowing what to do. Then they overcame their consternation and tried to get the Rebbe to change his mind.

"But you already agreed to come, Rebbe," said one.

"Why has the Rebbe changed his mind after he already gave his word?" asked another.

"Please come with us. We need you desperately," a third chimed in. "We are faced with an insurmountable problem which only the Rebbe can solve! We are depending on you!"

The Rebbe listened to their pleas with a sad expression, but he was firm in his decision. He would not go.

"I cannot! I cannot!" he finally blurted out. No one spoke. After a tense pause, the Rebbe continued, "I agreed to return with you to Yas. But when I was in my room, preparing to go, I overheard your conversation. After I heard someone suggest that I would stand to benefit from the trip, I was unable to bring myself to go. The thought slipped into my mind like poison and left a corrupting impression. The words 'a profitable trip' hammered at my brain. I had wanted to help you from the bottom of my heart, but my good intention was ruined by that evil thought. And so, I cannot bring myself to join you, no matter what. I cannot go!"

The delegation from Yas heard and understood. They were terribly disappointed over the failure of their mission, but they could not help admiring the Rebbe's exalted righteousness. They had themselves witnessed that all his actions were done with pure intention, free of any taint whatsoever. He was so cautious that when the question of the slightest personal gain intruded, he was prepared to disappoint a distinguished delegation to which he had given his word, rather than do something contrary to his conscience. For the Rebbe, a good deed had to be perfect.

They returned to Yas without R' Avraham David. But, before leaving Butchatch, they received his advice on their intricate matter and were able to put it to good use upon their return.

Reviewing Chovas Halevavos

R' Avraham David's amazing diligence in study was apparent even in his childhood.

When Avraham David was ten, his future father-in-law, R' Tzvi Hirsh Karo, author of *Neta Sha'ashuim*, wished to invite him to his home for a *yom tov*, to enjoy his brilliant company, for Avraham David charmed all his beholders with his intelligence.

R' Tzvi Hirsh sent a special messenger to convey his invitation and to accompany the young boy on the journey.

The family agreed and the two set out. Along the way, the sky suddenly grew dark and a torrent of rain poured down upon them.

The passengers in the open wagon were soaked through and through. They crept under anything at hand, be it a coat or blanket, to protect themselves from the violent downpour.

When the sudden shower was over, they all removed the coverings from their shoulders and heads, all, except for the young boy. He remained bundled under his coat, despite the change in weather.

His companion looked at him and noticed that his eyes were tightly shut. "Poor lad," he thought, "he must be exhausted by this trip. He is not used to traveling. I am glad that he is able to sleep."

They rode on and the boy 'slept' on. The older man looked at him from time to time and noticed that while his eyes were shut, his lips moved continuously.

He leaned over to hear what he was murmuring. The words were familiar. Was this not the text of a classic work?

Indeed, throughout the journey, Avraham David did not stop reciting the *Chovas Halevavos* from memory!

29 Tishrei

On this day, Shimon Hatzaddik passed away. He lived at the beginning of the period of the second Temple and was one of the last members of the *Anshei Knesses Hagedolah*, the Great Assembly.

The Sage in Black

Shimon Hatzaddik served as the *kohen gadol* in the *Beis Hamikdash* for forty years. Throughout this period, great miracles occurred in his merit.

In his final year, he predicted his death. At the beginning of the year, he said, "This year I will die."

"How do you know?" he was asked.

"Every other year when I performed the *Yom Kippur* service in the *Beis Hamikdash*, I was visited by an old man dressed in white. He entered and left together with me. This year, on *Yom Kippur*, the old man was dressed in black. He entered with me, but he did not leave with me."

Immediately after *Succos*, Shimon Hatzaddik became ill. He lay on his sickbed for seven days and then departed from this world (*Yoma 39a*).

The cave in which Shimon Hatzaddik is buried

Shimon Hatzaddik was buried in a cave in Jerusalem. This site has attracted thousands upon thousands of Jews over the years, and, to this very day, they come to pray and seek Heavenly mercy, especially on the anniversary of Shimon Hatzaddik's death.

This is the first day of *Rosh Chodesh Cheshvan*. The construction of the first *Beis Hamikdash* was completed in this month in 2934 after the Creation (826 B.C.E.).

Built in Wisdom

*W*hen Shlomo Hamelech was about to build the *Beis Hamikdash*, he sent messengers to Pharaoh, king of Egypt, requesting skilled workmen.

Pharaoh read Shlomo Hamelech's letter and an evil idea hatched in his mind. He planned to sabotage the building of the Temple.

Pharaoh gathered all the advisers and astrologers in his empire and told them to prepare a list of the skilled workmen who were fated to die in the coming year.

They followed his instructions and soon presented him with a list of all the skilled artisans destined to die shortly. Pharaoh summoned these men and sent them to Shlomo Hamelech.

Pharaoh gloated inwardly. He congratulated himself upon his cleverness and waited eagerly to see what would happen.

When the workers arrived from Egypt, Shlomo Hamelech saw at once, in his wisdom, that these men were all destined to die before long. He realized that this was how Pharaoh sought to foil the construction of the *Beis Hamikdash*.

Not to be outwitted, Shlomo Hamelech distributed a set of shrouds to each man and sent them back to their master with this message:

"Do you lack shrouds to bury your dead? I hereby return your men and send you their shrouds."

Cheshvan

R' Chaim Vital, the foremost disciple of the Ari Hakadosh and one of the greatest of Kabbalists, was born on this day in 5303 (1542). R' Chaim Vital died on the thirtieth of *Nisan* in 5380 (1620).

The Waters of the Kinneres and the Water of Gichon

When R' Chaim Vital came to the Ari Hakadosh to study Kabbalah, the Ari took him to T'veryah. Master and disciple reached the shores of the Kinneres. The Ari filled a cup with its water and gave it to R' Chaim to drink.

"This water comes from Miriam's Well," said the Ari, "from the rock which, through the merit of Miriam Haneviyah, supplied water to the Israelites throughout their forty-year sojourn in the desert. This water has a special property and will endow you with the capacity to study Kabbalah and to absorb it."

As soon as R' Chaim swallowed the water from Miriam's Well, his eyes were opened and he was able to understand many mystic secrets which had evaded him before. From then on, Kabbalah found a sanctuary within him.

The Chida (R' Chaim Yosef David Azulai) relates the following in his biographical work *Shem Hagedolim*:

During the time of the Ari, Jerusalem was ruled by a gentile governor. Water had always been scarce in Jerusalem and this ruler wished to create a steady supply into the city. He investigated the matter and learned that during the era of Chizkiyahu, the Gichon spring had flowed from the *Beis Hamikdash* and provided water for all the inhabitants. Chizkiyahu had stopped up the spring during his war with Sancheriv to prevent the enemy from seizing it.

When the governor heard this, he assembled his advisers and asked them how this spring could be found and released.

They thought and thought. Then one man arose and said, "The Jews have a saint by the name of R' Chaim Vital. He has the power to find the well and liberate its waters."

The governor summoned R' Chaim and ordered him to find the spring. "If you don't," he said, "you shall be put to death."

R' Chaim was reluctant to obey the governor. When he saw that his life was at stake, he prayed and, using holy Names known to him through Kabbalah, he made himself invisible and transported himself to Damascus, far from the governor's reach.

That night, the Ari appeared to R' Chaim in a dream and said, "How unfortunate it is that you failed to obey the governor's request. This was your chance to repair Chizkiyahu Hamelech's mistake. He should never have stopped up the Gichon. Had you uncovered it, you would have hastened the Redemption."

"Should I return to Jerusalem and do so now?" he asked.

"The opportunity has passed," replied the Ari. "Alas, it is too late now."

R' Yosef Zundel of Salant passed away in Jerusalem in 5626 (1865) on the evening of this day. He was one of those who had great influence on R' Yisrael of Salant, the founder of the *mussar* movement. R' Yosef Zundel was noted for his exceeding modesty.

Let Them Have Their Fun

A group of rich merchants was making its way by carriage to the big city. One of the passengers stuck out like a sore thumb. Unlike the others, who were dressed in expensive suits and thick fur coats, this man wore the dress of the poorest of paupers. Everyone took him for a beggar. How were they to know that he was none other than R' Yosef Zundel of Salant, who always wore simple, threadbare clothing? He looked so poor that no one ever dreamed that he was a famous scholar.

The carriage traveled along, bearing its passengers to their destination. The businessmen, having exhausted the topic of finance and business, began to use their biting tongues on the poor man sitting in their midst. "How many pennies did you collect today?" asked one, mockingly.

"Where is your luggage?" said another, with a sneer.

Each added his own comment, each vying with the next to make his jibe sharper and cleverer.

The shabbily dressed man did not react. He sat in his place, hearing the remarks directed at him, but maintaining his silence.

With nightfall, the carriage reached a wayside inn and stopped. All the passengers descended and entered the warm inn. R' Yosef Zundel entered as well and turned to say the evening prayers. He, then, took out some bread from his small satchel, dipped it in salt, and, after finishing this skimpy meal, curled up on a bench in a corner.

The rich merchants asked the innkeeper to prepare a sumptuous meal, for they were hungry. He laid out a lavish dinner and served wines and other expensive drinks. After they had stuffed themselves full, they suddenly remembered their poor fellow traveler. "Where's our friend, the beggar?" they asked.

They quickly discovered him sleeping peacefully upon a hard bench.

"Look! He's sleeping like a baby," cried one rich man.

"He must have been very tired."

A third approached the sleeping man and tugged playfully at his beard and long sidelocks.

R' Yosef Zundel awoke, but did not open his eyes. At once, he understood what was taking place. "Let them have their fun," he thought to himself, pretending to be asleep. "What do I care, as long as they enjoy themselves."

The merchants continued to amuse themselves at R' Yosef Zundel's expense, one yanking at his beard, another pulling at a sleeve, and all of them joking and laughing merrily.

Some time after the incident, R' Yosef Zundel happened to pass through the town where the group of businessmen lived.

The townspeople knew in advance of his visit and went out to greet the famous man. His erstwhile traveling companions were among them.

As soon as they caught sight of the visitor, they became

panic stricken. They began trembling with fear. "That is the very Jew whom we once teased so cruelly," they whispered to one another. "We must ask his forgiveness."

They approached him, heads bowed, and murmured ashamedly, "Forgive us, master. We wish to apologize for our disgraceful behavior. We took you for a beggar and did not dream that you were a noted scholar."

"I bear you no ill will," said R' Yosef Zundel. "It is all the same to me. In fact, I didn't mind one bit, seeing how you enjoyed yourselves, at the time. But I do have a request to make: From now on, be careful in your treatment of a poor Jew."

"Thank You" and not "Pardon"

Upon his ascent to Jerusalem, R' Yosef Zundel settled in the Churvah section of the Old City.

There was a water cistern in the courtyard adjoining his apartment. A water carrier would draw water from it and deliver it to his steady customers. Once, a woman came to the yard with an empty pail. She looked high and low for the water carrier, but he was nowhere about. Then she caught sight of R' Yosef Zundel leaving his house in his shabby clothing. She mistook him for a common person who earned his living by doing menial odd jobs.

"Can you draw two pails of water for me?" she asked, certain that he would be glad to earn a few pennies for this task. "But forgive me, for I don't have any money to pay you now. I'll pay you the next time I come."

"Never mind," said the man. "I'll fill your pails without pay. I trust that I will be repaid for my effort." He took the two pails, filled them to the top, and gave them to the woman.

"Thank you very much!" she called after him, but he had already disappeared through the archway.

A few days later she returned with her two empty pails and a few pennies to cover her debt. She searched for R' Yosef Zundel but could not find him. After describing him to several people, she learned that her 'water carrier' had been none other than the righteous R' Yosef Zundel.

When she realized this, she was overcome with sorrow. "How could I have bothered such a holy man with a menial task like that!" she asked herself, wretchedly. She went off to ask the *tzaddik* for his forgiveness.

"Rebbe," she said, when she found him, "I had no idea who you were. Please forgive me. I would never have asked you to toil for me had I known that you were R' Yosef Zundel."

"Forgive you? What for?" he replied. "On the contrary, you supplied me with a *mitzvah*. I am the richer for having helped you; I should thank you!"

R' Yisrael of Ruzhin passed away on this day in 5611 (1850). R' Yisrael was the founder of many illustrious chasidic dynasties. He was born on the third of *Tishrei*, 5557 (1796) and, already in his childhood, was outstanding in his piety.

A Convincing Argument

When R' Yisrael of Ruzhin turned thirteen, he celebrated his *bar mitzvah* with a feast attended by many famous Jewish personalities. One of the rabbis turned to the young Yisrael and asked, "You know that the good inclination joins a person when he becomes of age, at thirteen. Yet, his evil inclination is with him right from birth. Tell me, how were you able to stand up to him all these years without the aid of your good inclination?"

Without hesitation, the lad replied, "Whenever my *yetzer hara* tried to tempt me to sin, I put him off with a convincing argument."

"And what was that?"

"I told him that the law forbids a judge to hear the arguments of one of the parties in a case if the other one is not present. So he would have to wait until I turned thirteen and my good inclination will be able to refute his persuasive arguments."

Calculations of a Five-Year-Old

hen R' Yisrael of Ruzhin was five years old, his father entered his room and beheld a strange sight. Little Srulik, as he was called, was pacing the floor and sobbing bitterly. He wrung his hands in deep distress.

"What is the matter, my son?" asked the father, R' Shalom, in alarm.

The little boy looked up with reddened eyes and said hoarsely, "Oh, Father, I am counting how many times I raised my two hands today for reasons other than the glory of *Hashem*."

On this day in 4926 (1165), R' Moshe ben Maimon, the Rambam, reached Jerusalem for a visit. Having arrived safely, he resolved to celebrate this date each year (see the Rambam's letter in *Sefer Hacharedim*).

He Saw Red

The Rambam lived in Egypt for many years. In addition to being acclaimed for his greatness in the world of Torah, he gained fame as an exceptional physician. Everyone hailed his expertise in medicine, and it was no great wonder that the sultan asked him to serve as the court physician in his palace in Cairo.

There were many other doctors serving at court, each well known for his skills. The Rambam stood out above them all and enjoyed the sultan's esteem and affection.

The other doctors envied the Rambam his favored position. It aroused their jealousy that the sultan should value his Jewish doctor more than the Moslem doctors, who were of his own faith. They sought every opportunity to discredit the Rambam before the sultan. They slandered him and schemed against him constantly. But the sultan was not fooled by their evil words and ignored them. He knew that the Rambam was superior to them and that they were jealous of his success.

The more they defamed him, the higher rose the sultan's

The Rambam

opinion of the Rambam. And the more the sultan honored the Rambam, the greater grew his rivals' hatred. They would not give up. Their envy aroused them to furious and frantic efforts to ruin the Rambam's reputation.

Once, when the court physicians came to the sultan with a new vicious tale, the sultan's patience burst. "You are always claiming that you are better doctors than the Rambam," he said. "Very well. Let us put your knowledge to the test. If you can convince me that you are more skilled than he is, I will believe you."

"Give us until tomorrow, Your Excellency!" they said joyfully.

On the following day, they arrived at court with a blind man.

"Your Excellency," they said. "We have brought the proof you asked. This man is blind from birth. He never saw the light of day. But we, with our superior skill, can heal his blindness and make him see."

The sultan was duly impressed by such a claim. The Rambam, who was present, maintained that this was impossible. "A person who was born blind cannot have sight given to him," he said emphatically.

"You are unable to grant him sight," they mocked the Rambam, "but we can. Watch and see."

One of the physicians applied an ointment to the man's eyes. Everyone waited with bated breaths. Would the man see? Would the Rambam be proven wrong for the first time?

After a few moments, the man opened his eyes and burst out excitedly, "I can see! I can see!"

Before anyone could say a word, the Rambam approached him and waved a handkerchief before the 'blind' man's eyes. "What color is this?" he asked.

"Red!" said the man, joyfully.

The Rambam turned to the sultan and his courtiers and said, "It is perfectly clear that this is a hoax. The man was never blind and certainly not from birth. For if he had never seen before, how could he have recognized the color?"

Ashamed at having been exposed in their chicanery, the physicians slunk out of the room, leaving the sultan and his favorite doctor behind.

R' Yisrael Salanter was born on the evening of this day in 5570 (1809). R' Yisrael is known as the founder of the *mussar* movement. He died on the twenty-fifth of *Shevat*, 5643 (1883).

R' Yisrael Asleep

R' Yisrael Salanter spent most of the twenty-four hours of the day in service to *Hashem*, ignoring his own personal needs. He lived for *Hashem* and for his fellow man and gave them all he had of his time and his strength.

Small wonder that when his closer disciples once found R' Yisrael fast asleep, they made sure that utter silence would reign in the house so that he would not be disturbed. "This time," they said, "no one is to wake him up. If someone comes to the door, we will try to help him ourselves or else, tell him to wait."

Everyone walked about on tiptoe and spoke in a whisper. The silence was suddenly broken by loud fast-paced steps. A man entered and, as one who knew his goal, strode directly towards R' Yisrael's study. Another moment and he would knock.

"Sir!" whispered the disciples loudly. "One moment! Where do you think you are going?"

"Where am I going?" he cried back. "This is R' Yisrael's door, isn't it? I need a letter of recommendation from him for my business."

"You must wait until he wakes up," said the disciples.

Without saying a word, the man left.

R' Yisrael awoke a short while later, having taken no more than a brief nap. Soon, the house was abustle with the usual activity. R' Yisrael learned that while he had been asleep, a man had come to ask for a letter of recommendation.

"Why didn't you wake me?" asked R' Yisrael. "How did you have the heart to send away a Jew who needed help?"

R' Yisrael did not rest until he had discovered the name of the man and his address. He donned his coat and hat and left the house to find him, ask his forgiveness and fulfill his request.

R' Yisrael Awake

R' Yitzchak Maltzan, a famous disciple of R' Yisrael, had a room in his master's house. Both student and master had keys to the door of the house, so that each could come and go freely at will.

One evening, R' Yitzchak said to R' Yisrael, "Rebbe, I have an urgent matter to tend to. I won't be back until late at night."

R' Yisrael did not reply; he was engrossed in his study and merely nodded, while continuing to pore over the books piled high on his table.

No one else was home at the time, an unusual situation. And so, there was no one to distract R' Yisrael as he sat at his table and studied, undisturbed. After many hours, he got up, made himself a cup of tea and returned to the table. His eye happened to fall upon a key lying among the many books.

"This must be R' Yitzchak's key," he thought. "He must have forgotten it when he rushed out. When he returns home late at night and sees that the key is missing, he will not knock on the door for fear of awakening me. If I know him, he will choose to remain standing outside the door all night. But it is so cold and windy tonight."

R' Yisrael could not bear the thought of his beloved disciple spending the night on the doorstep. He got up, put on his coat and went outside. He walked up and down the front yard in the cold, waiting for R' Yitzchak.

The cold became more intense, from moment to moment. The hands of the clock advanced and it was already past midnight. Only then were footsteps heard; R' Yitzchak was returning home.

Without even noticing his master, he walked up to the door, felt in his pocket for the key and stopped short. The wide large pocket was empty. He searched his other pockets, but the key was not there, either.

"I must have forgotten it," he murmured. "I dare not knock on the door and wake up R' Yisrael. I have no choice but to wait the night out here, or else go to the *beis medrash*."

Still thinking about what to do, he heard footsteps. He drew back in fear. "Who is it?" he asked in quavering tones.

"Is that you, R' Yitzchak?" came his master's familiar voice. "You forgot your key on the table. I came out to let you in; I knew that you would not want to wake me up."

Tzidkiyahu Hamelech was blinded on this day. Tzidkiyahu was the last king of the Davidic dynasty. The event occurred in the year 3308 after the Creation (452 B.C.E.) *(Shulchan Aruch: Orach Chaim, siman 580b, according to the Magen Avraham)*.

A King, not a Deer

The capture of Tzidkiyahu Hamelech after the destruction of the first *Beis Hamikdash* brought an end to the dynasty of the House of David.

The *Midrash* relates: When Nevuchadnezzar's army invaded Jerusalem, Tzidkiyahu Hamelech fled the city with many of his soldiers through a cave running all the way to Jericho. (This very cave can be seen today; its opening is to the left of the Damascus Gate in the wall of the Old City.)

While Tzidkiyahu and his men were fleeing through the underground cave, *Hashem* caused a deer to run above it. The Babylonian soldiers pursued it, hoping to hunt it down. In their pursuit of the deer, they reached the far end of the cave, near Jericho, just in time to see Tzidkiyahu and his men emerge.

They seized him and brought him before Nevuchadnezzar, king of Babylonia, who had his eyes put out. Tzidkiyahu was led to Babylonia in iron shackles and died in prison.

In *Eretz Yisrael*, people begin to say, *"Vesein tal umatar* — give dew and rain,"* in the fourth blessing of the *shemoneh esrei*.

Noise on the Rooftops

Towards the end of his days, R' Avraham Dov, rabbi of Everitch, went up to *Eretz Yisrael*, choosing to settle in Tzefas.

His first days were difficult and dismaying. He could not acclimate himself to the place or the people, nor did he feel the special sanctity of the Holy Land. Indeed, it is written in holy works that this is one of the trials which worthy men are subjected to upon coming to the Holy Land; they do not feel any particular holiness when they first come. Only later does Heaven open their eyes and make them sensitive to the sanctity of the land.

And so it was with R' Avraham Dov. He thought, "Why must I suffer such pain and disappointment? I left my family behind in Everitch. They long to see me. And my disciples pine to hear my teachings again. Why must I remain here, alone, and suffer?" He reached the difficult decision to return to Everitch, to his family and followers.

He prepared for his return to the Diaspora. It was the beginning of *Cheshvan*.

On the sixth of *Cheshvan*, when R' Avraham Dov was on his way to the synagogue for *minchah*, he heard noises from the rooftops. "What is the matter? What is happening?" he cried.

"Oh, don't you know?" he was told. "In Tzefas, people store various food supplies and household items on the flat roofs. They also hang laundry and do other chores there. The women are now taking down the food and things from the rooftops."

"Why now?"

"So that nothing will get wet and ruined from the rain."

R' Avraham Dov looked up at the sky. It was blue down to the horizon, without a speck of cloud. "It doesn't look as if it's about to rain to me. Why is everyone suddenly so concerned?"

"Have you forgotten? Tonight is the seventh of *Cheshvan*. Tonight we begin to say, '*Vesein tal umatar*,' in the prayers.

"You see, we trust that *Hashem* will hear our prayers and will send rain, as we ask. And so, in order to be prepared, we must take down the perishables from the rooftops lest they spoil."

R' Avraham Dov was deeply moved by their simple, trusting words and their wholesome faith in the Almighty. "I am beginning to see the heights attained by these wonderful people and their unshakable faith. They are holy and pure. I shall remain here in their midst, and consider it a privilege to do so."

He immediately broke off his preparations for the return 'home' to Everitch.

On this day, when we begin asking for rain, the *tzaddik* of Evertich first felt the special quality of *Eretz Yisrael* and its inhabitants. And with the passing of time, he grew spiritually, until he was able to genuinely appreciate the importance and uniqueness of the Holy Land. He later revealed all this to his followers in Tzefas.

R' Nachum of Horodna passed away on this day. R' Nachum, a great sage and worker of miracles, was also extremely humble. He declined all offers of positions as rabbi, and served as a simple *shammash* in Horodna, Lithuania. Despite this lowly post, he became famous as an exalted personality and a worker of miracles. R' Nachum of Horodna was born in 5572 (1812) and died in 5640 (1879).

Fire Insurance

A wealthy and propertied man once decided to take out a fire insurance policy to protect his home with its expensive furnishings and his other holdings. The insurance agent lived in Horodna, and he went there.

When he arrived, he saw R' Nachum passing through the market, collecting money for the poor. Having heard much about R' Nachum, the rich man approached him and said, "Honored rabbi, I have an urgent request."

"What is it, my friend?"

"I have come here to take out a large insurance policy against fire. I have set fifty rubles aside for that purpose. But seeing you, an idea struck me. If I give you the entire sum to distribute as you see fit among the poor, will you guarantee that no fire breaks out on my estate?"

HaGaon R' Nachum of Horodna

"Am I a substitute for *Hashem* that I can make such a promise?" said the *tzaddik* in surprise. "I cannot guarantee anything. But I can give you my blessing that the merit of your charity protect you from all harm, including fire."

The rich man was pleased with R' Nachum's blessing. He gave him the fifty rubles and returned home satisfied.

One summer day, many years after that encounter, the rich man awoke to the sound of crackling flames. Fire! Smoke filled his nostrils. He and his sons rushed out. The fire was in the direction of the warehouse where they stored barrels of whiskey.

"The roof of the whiskey warehouse is on fire!" they shouted. If it burned down, it would be a terrible loss. The stock was worth some ten thousand rubles — a fortune!

The entire village gathered at the site of the fire. People wrung their hands in distress, terrified that it would reach their homes. They brought buckets of water and poured them on the threatening flames.

"What if it spreads?"said one.

"It can burn the entire town down!" said another.

Meanwhile, the wealthy owner stood by, watching. He did not shout or weep. He did not wring his hands helplessly. Serene and calm, he said softly, "R' Nachum gave me his blessing that no fire would inflict damage upon my property. He will certainly stand by his promise."

The words were barely out of his mouth when a strong wind arose. It extinguished the fire in moments and the damage was superficial.

"Whoever saw it," the rich man would say, in the years to come, "can bear witness that it was an unnatural spectacle, a true miracle!"

R' Dov Berish Weidenfeld, rabbi of Tchebin, passed away on the evening of this day in 5726 (1965). He was one of the foremost Jewish leaders of our generation. R' Dov Berish was born on the fifth of *Shevat* in 5641 (1881), survived the Holocaust and immigrated to *Eretz Yisrael*, establishing his *yeshivah*, *Kochav MiYaakov*, in Jerusalem. This *yeshivah* has produced tens of thousands of outstanding Jews.

Travel Without Wheels?

Avehement political battle was waged in the State of Israel before *yeshivah* students were exempt from military duty. R' Dov Berish Weidenfeld took an active part in the fight, in the course of which he met with many military figures.

They explained their position: The country was surrounded on all sides by enemies. Her security was threatened. It was necessary, they said, to increase the ranks of the army to defend our difficult borders. Manpower was of the essence; every *yeshivah* student counted.

When they had finished presenting their case, he said, "I would like to tell you a true story:

"A heavily loaded wagon was once being pulled up a steep hill. It made slow progress. The tired horses exerted themselves to their utmost, but when they were half way up, they stopped. They could not continue.

"Seeing their plight, the driver decided to lighten their load. He jumped off his seat and began throwing out bundle after bundle. Every few moments, he prodded the horses to resume their haul, but they stubbornly refused to budge and he continued to cast out the packages.

"Most of the wagon had been emptied, but still the horses would not move. In desperation, he began removing the heavy wagon wheels. 'They are made of iron and must be very heavy,' he thought, foolishly. 'Without them, the horses will finally be able to pull the wagon to the top of the hill'."

R' Dov Berish fixed a stern gaze upon the military men seated opposite him. "This is what you are attempting to do, as well —to dismantle the wagon wheels. You wish to conscript the *yeshivah* students, in whose merit the world exists, but you fail to realize that these selfsame students are making the wagon go. They mobilize the Heavenly Chariot of Divine Providence. As King David says in *Tehillim*, 'Our feet stood at the gates of Jerusalem.' Our Sages interpret this verse as follows: 'Our feet stood' — firm in battle, due to — 'the gates of Jerusalem' — those who devote their lives to the study of Torah in the Holy City of Jerusalem."

Another Participant

A noted scholar became seriously ill. Since he was indigent, several prominent people took up a collection to help him in his need. R' Dov Berish Weidenfeld learned of it and that *Shabbos*, after prayers, he turned to one of the men involved

R' Dov Berish Weidenfeld, the Tchebiner Rav

and said, "I would like to have a part in this important *mitzvah*.

The man knew that the Rav himself was poor and replied that he only accepted large donations. "A person of his stature does not deserve petty funds."

"If that is the case, I am willing to give a sizable donation, too," said the Rav. He told the man to come to him on the following day to collect his pledge.

Knowing that the Rav did not have the means to give much, the man was evasive. He did not appear on Sunday or on Monday. On Tuesday, the Tchebiner Rav sent a messenger asking him to come. When he finally arrived, R' Dov Berish gave him a considerable sum. The man knew that it must represent a fortune for the Rav, and tried to refuse it.

"Let me tell you a true story," said R' Dov Berish. "R' Shlomo Kluger of Brody once visited R' Shalom of Belz and was accorded great honor. As he was about to leave, the Belzer Rebbe rushed forward to the vestibule to fetch his visitor's coat. 'What is this?' asked R' Shlomo, shocked, when the Rebbe handed him his coat. 'I wish the privilege of serving a Torah scholar!' exclaimed the Rebbe.

"The man for whom you are collecting is a rare personality. How many like him can we number in our generation? I consider it a great privilege to be allowed to help him in his need."

The Proof

The Chazon Ish was exceptionally meticulous and concerned when performing a *mitzvah*. Before *Pesach*, among other practices, he would gather all of his *sefarim* together and place them into a bookcase which he locked tightly for the duration of the Festival. He was afraid that some crumbs might have remained in the *sefarim* and gone undetected.

He reserved one *gemara* and several other volumes for his

use on *Pesach*, but these were first inspected page by page for any minute crumbs of *chametz*.

When the Chazon Ish received his copy of *Dovev Meisharim* by R' Dov Berish Weidenfeld, he included this among the few items that remained on his study table during *Pesach*.

The Rav of Tchebin learned of this and, in his humble way, made light of the honor, saying, "It only goes to show that the Chazon Ish does not study it throughout the year."

10 Cheshvan

R' Nachum of Chernobyl passed away on the evening of this day in 5558 (1797). R' Nachum, born in 5490 (1730), was the head of the illustrious Chernobyl dynasty and its many branches.

With All His Means

R' Nachum of Chernobyl was outstanding in his efforts to help his fellow man. He especially lavished charity upon the poor and would do anything to ease their plight. From time to time, R' Nachum would leave his home and travel among the towns and villages to seek out the downtrodden and unfortunate, and help them to the best of his ability.

His concern was not only the people's material needs, but also their spiritual poverty. At the towns and villages he visited, he would inquire whether there was a proper synagogue and *mikveh*, whether they lacked a school, or if the community could afford to keep a rabbi and *shochet*. If there was any particular communal need, he would set about filling it. He would raise funds and take the necessary steps to supply what was wanting, be it a rabbi, proper synagogue or the like.

R' Nachum once arrived in a remote town which lacked its own *mikveh*.

He immediately approached a wealthy acquaintance and follower with an unusual offer: "I am willing to sell you my portion in the World-to-Come in return for your building a *mikveh* in that remote town."

The man willingly agreed to such a bargain. The Rebbe's chasidim, however, were surprised at this transaction.

In answer to their questioning looks, the Rebbe said, "The Torah obligates us to 'love *Hashem* with all your heart, with all your soul and with all your might' (*Devarim 6:5*). Rashi explains 'all your might' to be 'your means,' that is, your money.

"I recite this verse twice daily, morning and evening. And I ask myself, 'How can a Jew like me, who does not have a penny to his name, fulfill this commandment?' How can I profess to love *Hashem* with all my money without lying to myself?

"But, if I do not own any money, I do possess something else of value, and that is a portion in the World-to-Come. There are people who are even willing to put a price on that possession. If so, I am obligated to sell this property by way of fulfilling my obligation of 'loving *Hashem* with all my might'!"

This is the anniversary of the death of Rachel Imeinu and also the birthday of Binyamin, since she died in childbirth. Rachel Imeinu died at the age of thirty-six. Binyamin died one hundred and nine years later.

On the Road to Beis Lechem

*W*hen Yaakov Avinu returned with his family from Lavan's house, he passed through Beis El in the Land of Canaan and from there, continued on to Chevron.

Along the way, his wife, Rachel, went into difficult labor and gave birth to Binyamin, dying in childbirth. She was buried in Beis Lechem. "And Yaakov erected a monument upon her grave, this is the monument of *kever Rachel* to this very day" (*Bereishis 35:16-20*).

The Tomb of Rachel has served our people as a prayer site throughout the generations. People are drawn here to pour out their hearts and invoke the merit of our Matriarch when they or their communities fall upon troubled times, especially on the eleventh of *Cheshvan*, the day of her death.

Rachel did not have the fortune to be buried in the *Me'aras Hamachpelah*, in Chevron, together with the other Matriarchs and Patriarchs. Yaakov Avinu decided to bury his favorite wife here, on the roadside, rather than in the ancestral

The tomb of Rachel Imeinu

grave in Chevron, for he saw in his Divine intuition that his sons would be driven from the Holy Land after the destruction of the *Beis Hamikdash*. On their way to

Babylonia, the exiles would pass along the road to Beis Lechem. He wanted Rachel to be buried here, so that she could intercede for them before the Almighty and ask for Heavenly protection and mercy for them.

During the Babylonian exile, Yirmeyahu would frequently come here to pray. He did not cease praying until he was promised that Israel would return from their exile.

Our Sages tell us as follows:

When the prophet Yirmeyahu saw the *Beis Hamikdash* in smoldering ruins and the people going into exile, he went and prostrated himself upon the graves of the *Avos* in the *Me'aras Hamachpelah* and wept, "Stand up, Patriarchs, and plead before the Almighty for your sons who are going into exile."

Avraham Avinu arose and beseeched the Almighty, "Master of the world! Why have You expelled my sons and delivered them to the nations? Why have You destroyed the *Beis Hamikdash*, the site where I bound up my son Yitzchak as a sacrifice to You?"

"Your sons have sinned and violated the commandments of the Torah," replied *Hashem*.

The other *Avos*, also, sought mercy for their children, but their prayers were similarly rejected.

When the exiles passed near Rachel's tomb on the road to Beis Lechem, Rachel came before *Hashem* and said, "Master of the world! It is known before You that Yaakov served my father Lavan seven years in order to marry me. When my wedding day arrived, my father led my sister to the *chupah* in my place. I did not envy my sister, nor expose my father's deception and embarrass her.

"And if I, a mortal of flesh and blood, ashes and dust, acted thus, You, the Everlasting G-d and Merciful King, should surely not be wrathful and envious."

Her heartfelt words aroused Heavenly compassion and

Hashem said, "For your sake, Rachel, will I return Israel to its borders."

Thus is it written in the Book of *Yirmeyahu*: "A voice is heard in the Heavens, a bitter mournful weeping. Rachel weeps over her sons; she refuses to be comforted" (31:14). And the prophet goes on to speak: "Thus says *Hashem*, 'Withhold your voice from weeping and your eyes from tears, for there is reward for your act . . . And there is hope for your future, and sons shall return to their border.' "

Rachel's tomb was a place of prayer for her son, Yosef, too. Here he poured forth his prayers and tears and found solace, as it is written in *Sefer Hayashar*:

When Yosef was sold to the Yishmaelites, he was led past his mother's grave at Beis Lechem. Yosef rushed up to the tomb and falling upon it, he cried out, weeping, "Mother! Mother who bore me! Wake up and see your son! Look upon him. See how they have cast me forth and sold me as a slave; they have separated me from my father and there is no one to take pity . . ."

Then, a tearful voice reached his ears. "My son, my son, Yosef! I hear the sound of your weeping and the sound of your cries. I see your tears and I know full well of your suffering. My son, I ache for you. Your pain compounds my own suffering. And now, my son Yosef, trust in *Hashem* and have faith in Him. Do not fear, for He is with you and He will protect you from all harm. Rise, my son, and go down to Egypt with these masters. Do not fear — for *Hashem* is with you!"

Sarah Imeinu died in this month (*Midrash Rabbah Esther* 7:13) at the age of one hundred and twenty-seven. She is buried in the *Me'aras Hamachpelah* in Chevron.

Happiness Brings the Blessing

The daughter of R' Shmuel of Kaminka, one of the disciples of the Baal Shem Tov, was childless for many years. Whenever she heard that a *tzaddik* was coming to her city, she would not rest until she had received his blessing for children.

R' Refael of Barshad, who was especially known for the wonders he wrought, once came to Kaminka. She went to him at once and pleaded that he bless her, too.

He duly blessed her, but added, "You should know that joy is a *segulah* for bearing children."

She later told her father, R' Shmuel, what the *tzaddik* from Barshad had said and he, in turn, replied, "True. We find it in the *chumash*, the Prophets and the Sacred Writings.

"In the Torah it is written: 'And Sarah laughed' (*Bereishis 18:12*). When Sarah was told of the forthcoming birth of a son, she laughed, and because of her joy, she was able to conceive.

"In Prophets we find: 'Rejoice, O barren one who never

bore' (*Yeshayahu 54:1*). The barren woman need only rejoice and exult and *Hashem* will quickly send her rescue and deliverance.

"Finally, in the Sacred Writings it is written: 'Who causes the barren woman to sit as the happy mother of sons' (*Tehillim 113:9*). *Hashem* transforms the barren woman into the mother of sons by virtue of her happiness in her lot."

His daughter listened attentively, but was troubled and said, "If Sarah laughed because joy is conducive to childbearing, why was *Hashem* angry with her, asking why she had laughed?"

R' Shmuel replied, "A *segulah* is an aid, or charm. One uses it to help make the blessing of a *tzaddik* more effective. But this is unnecessary when the blessing comes directly from *Hashem*. And here, He Himself promised Sarah that she would bear a son. The *segulah* was superfluous, and she did not need the help of joy and laughter."

In this month, we hope and pray for rain.

Rain — for the Worthy

ain had not yet fallen in Tzipori, in the Galilee, where R' Chanina bar Chama lived. R' Chanina declared a public fast, but, still, no rain fell.

There was a drought in the south, too, and R' Yehoshua ben Levi, who lived there, also decreed a fast for those who lived in the area. Their prayers were answered and blessed rain fell.

When the people of Tzipori heard of this, they said, "R' Yehoshua ben Levi was successful in bringing rain to the south. Why couldn't R' Chanina bar Chama do so for us in Tzipori?"

It was decided to proclaim another public fast day in Tzipori. In order that it should be effective, R' Chanina asked R' Yehoshua to come and join them in prayer. This time, both *tzaddikim* prayed for rain, but no rain fell in Tzipori.

When he saw this, R' Chanina gathered the townspeople and said, "Now you see that it was not R' Yehoshua ben Levi who brought rain in the south or R' Chanina who withheld the rain from Tzipori. Rain fell in the south because the people's hearts are tender there and when they heard a call to repentance, they listened and acted. But your hearts are hard.

You hear words of rebuke which should arouse you, but remain impassive. You do not repent."

R' Chanina then raised his eyes toward Heaven. The skies were totally blue with not a single cloud in sight. "Is it still so?" he asked. At once, clouds gathered and rain fell (*Yerushalmi, Taanis 3:4*).

14 Cheshvan

Matisyahu the *Kohen Gadol* passed away on the evening of this day in the year 3622 after Creation (138 B.C.E.)

Standing in the Breach

*M*atisyahu the *Kohen Gadol* was one of the great heroes of Jewish history. He fought the Greeks and the Jewish Hellenists and succeeded in preserving Torah for Jewry.

Matisyahu in his generation, and Jewish leaders in all generations, have protected the fortress of Torah and *mitzvos* lest it be breached in any way, either by the gentile enemy, or the enemy within, who rose up from our own ranks. With the help of *Hashem*, they succeeded in overcoming the threats of evil schemers and the fortress has remained intact.

Kosher Meat in a Treife Pot

A well-known *darshan* (speaker) was reported not to live up to his own teachings. It was said that he no longer observed the commandments and was not fit to address devout audiences.

That speaker once came to Brisk, where R' Chaim Soloveitchik was rabbi. R' Chaim soon learned about his questionable behavior and issued instructions not to allow the man to speak in public.

The *darshan* came before R' Chaim to complain. "Come and hear what I have to say," he said, "and you will see that it is kosher, beyond reproach. My talks are based completely on the written and oral traditions of the Torah and well spiced with excerpts from *mussar* works, studied by our people for generations. What fault can you possibly find? Why do you forbid me to speak in public?"

"Even if what you say is perfectly kosher, you will not make me change my mind," replied R' Chaim. "Brisk is a city of decent and devout Jews who should not be exposed to evil influences. Meat, that was slaughtered by an expert *shochet* and properly soaked and salted with the utmost care and safeguards, immediately becomes *treife* if it is cooked in a pot which is not kosher."

Selling or Selling Out

During R' Chaim's tenure as rabbi of Brisk, a Jew was appointed to a high government office and converted to Christianity. Nevertheless, he continued to favor Jews and ease the oppression they suffered at the hands of the authorities.

For his seventieth birthday, the official was swamped with letters of congratulation from all over the country. Even well-known rabbis sent him their greetings in appreciation for all he had done for Jewry.

The community of Brisk, also, wished to acknowledge the occasion with a letter of blessing. But R' Chaim was strongly opposed. "We must not make any contact with apostates," he ruled, "even if they help Jews."

A report of this statement reached the ears of the official. He sent a one-line letter to R' Chaim of Brisk that read, "And Yosef recognized his brothers, but they did not recognize him" (*Bereishis 42:8*). He meant that he, Joseph, had not forgotten the Jews even though he had converted, while the Jews, namely R' Chaim, treated him as though they had never known him.

R' Chaim's reply was just as terse. He wrote: "There, Yosef's brothers sold Yosef, while here, Yosef, himself, sold out; he betrayed his brothers."

R' Avraham Yeshayahu Karelitz, the Chazon Ish, passed away on this day in 5714 (1954). He was one of the most famous personalities of his time. Many visit his graveside, especially on his *yahrzeit*.

What Happened to "Your Sons"?

A simple Jew came to the Chazon Ish. His wife, he said, had given birth to several children over the years, but none of them had survived beyond the first week.

"You must change the *mezuzos* in your house," advised the Chazon Ish. "Buy new *mezuzah* parchments which have been written with care by a scribe who is trustworthy and affix them on your doorposts."

The Chazon Ish had a close acquaintance help the man, who was unlearned, purchase high-quality parchments. He wanted the matter to be taken care of properly.

Upon arriving at the man's house, the two removed the old *mezuzah* at the front door. To their amazement, upon unrolling it, they saw that the word *"beneichem* — your sons" was so riddled with holes as to be illegible!

Discreet Language

I t was noon in the Karelitz household. Everyone sat quietly about the table. The gentle click of dishes and clink of cutlery mingled with pleasant talk revolving about Torah.

This house was unique in that Torah was the topic of conversation at every single meal. The family absorbed this spiritual fare along with the food on their plates.

The father was engaged in a fascinating conversation with his sons. The mother, who had finished serving, had taken her place at the table and was listening to their talk.

She looked happily about and her eyes came to rest upon seven-year-old Avraham Yeshayahu who sat in silence, not touching the food before him.

"Avraham Yeshayahu," she said in concern, "what is the matter with you? Why aren't you eating your meal?"

Fixing his eyes on the ground, he replied, apologetically, "Mother, they forgot to give me a fork."

She hurried into the kitchen to fetch a fork. To her surprise, she discovered a portion of meat still in the pot. She returned to the table with the fork and realized that that must be Avraham Yeshayahu's portion, for his plate was empty. Not only had he not received a fork, he had not been served any food, either!

The youngster had not said a word to his mother, for fear of insulting her in some minute measure, or calling her to task for having forgotten him. He had preferred to remain silent rather than hurt her feelings.

Even when his mother had seen that he was not eating, he still had taken care not to offend her. Instead of complaining

R' Avraham Yeshayahu Karelitz, the author of "Chazon Ish"

that he had not received his portion, he had mentioned the lesser fault, of not having a fork, leaving the rest up to her own understanding.

Avraham Yeshayahu was finally served his portion, albeit late. His mother had learned that, young as he was, he was already great in character, and that his words were weighed with wisdom and righteousness on a delicate balance, to express exactly what must be said.

How to Study Torah

The *beis medrash* of Kosova always teemed with people. The sound of Torah reverberated from its walls at all hours of the day and night. But one sound did not blend with the rest; it stood out from the familiar voices.

It was an other-worldly sound.

Strong, forceful, it sought to storm its way through the sealed gates of the Torah. It was a sound that burst forth from three stalwart young men of sublime character who pursued their study for hours on end. Their heartwarming voices had poured into the ears of the townsmen of Kosova for several months.

Who were these exceptional youths?

They were the pride and joy of Kosova: R' Avraham Yeshayahu Karelitz, who would become famous as the Chazon Ish; his brother, Meir Karelitz, and their good friend. The three had agreed to study two daily sessions together. Only two sessions, but what quality-packed minutes and hours they contained! Each could easily compare with tens of hours spent in study by their peers, both in scope and depth. Each session was six hours long, with not one of the three hundred and sixty minutes wasted! Nonstop. They made a small recess between one session and the next to refresh their minds and iron out the kinks in their muscles in preparation for the next session of six hours.

This taxing schedule lasted over a long period of time, for they wished to climb higher and higher on the heights of Torah.

Anyone who had happened to come across them accidently would have witnessed a moving scene: Three young men seated at the table, their faces aflame. The words issuing from their mouths seemed like tongues of fire. Faces flushed from effort, eyes burning with the blaze of discovered truth, their appearance bespoke an unquenchable desire to plumb the depths of Torah at all costs. In their quest for understanding, they seemed like drowning men at sea, swimming with all their might to reach land. At such a moment, all of their thoughts focus on one thing: to live! This is how those three youths looked when they swam for their lives in the sea of the Talmud, grasping at every plank, every platform of reasoning. Their minds whirled; they gasped for the breath of truth. Was this the genuine thing, they would ask themselves over and over when clarifying a difficult topic, or were they being deceived by an errant hint of falsehood? They tested and examined their logic from all angles.

"Implant the Torah of truth into our hearts," their lips whispered softly into the melody of their study.

They sat for hours on end, these three, as if there were no beginning and no end.

The very walls of the *beis medrash* marveled at their diligence. From where did these sweet young boys derive their staying power?

Six hours passed, minute after minute, without a wasted moment. And afterwards, the boys arose to stretch a bit. After a brief pause during which they managed some nourishment and a short walk, they returned to their study bench, refreshed and invigorated, as if they had just awoken from a night's sleep.

They began their second session full of enthusiasm. The words gushed forth from their lips and filled the room with holy breath.

They would first study the text of the *gemara* and then

continue with *Rashi*, the *Tosafos* and the other *rishonim*, the early commentaries.

Occasionally, the *gemara* echoed hollowly. They could not fathom its words. Then their eyes would shut and the sweet melody would cease. Furrows would crease their foreheads, testifying to intensive mental exertion. The harder they tried to understand, the more confused they became. Soon they would sink into an obscure fog. But that must not happen!

"What shall we do? Whence shall come our help?"

They would seek the answer from one another and then, unanimously, turn to the Omniscient Who dispensed of His wisdom to mankind. Their *gemaras* would close. Each would take up a *Tehillim*. Each would retire to a corner and, tears flowing, would pray that He enlighten their eyes in Torah and dissolve the barrier that stood between them and their subject.

They hoped that their tears would erode the stone barrier of misunderstanding, just as R' Akiva had observed water eroding a stone.

Their hearts were broken. What was the use of studying if they lacked understanding?

"Master of the world!" they cried, "Merciful and compassionate Father! Almighty One! Look upon our tears and do not ignore our pleas. Grant us understanding to comprehend Your Torah, for our fountains have dried up and we are lost without Your help. Do not turn us away empty handed. Do not remove Your Divine spirit from us."

Their eyes awash with tears, they would return to their places and make another attempt at fathoming the words. Perhaps their prayers had been received. Perhaps they had been granted enlightenment. The *gemara* would again be opened and a hopeful, sprightly melody would spring to their lips. They would attack their problem again, and if need be, again . . .

Then, slowly, the fog would be dispelled and the light would shine through between the words.

When they finally understood the subject thoroughly, they would exult as if they had fished up a rare gem from the sea of the Talmud. Their joy would surge and overflow. This was true bliss, the joy of a *mitzvah*, a victory at sea. "I rejoice over Your sayings like the finder of great spoils!" they would quote, feelingly.

They followed this practice over a long period. The three persevered at their self-imposed schedule and succeeded in reaching peaks of glorious achievement.

16 Cheshvan

R' Menachem Mendel of Kosov, who founded several chasidic dynasties and was hailed as a holy figure, passed away on the evening of this day in 5586 (1825). He was born in 5528 (1768).

Ignoring the Critics

One of his fellow townsmen was violently opposed to R' Menachem Mendel, Rebbe of Kosov. Whenever the opportunity arose, he would denounce him and seek to interfere with his many vital works.

One day, to the great surprise of the Rebbe's household, the man knocked on R' Menachem Mendel's door, asking to speak to the Rebbe.

The *shammash* showed him in and he told the Rebbe of his bitter financial situation. "My daughter has come of age, but I have no means to marry her off. Tell me, Rebbe, how I am supposed to solve this problem?"

"How much money do you need to provide a dowry?" asked the Rebbe.

He mentioned a large sum. Without hesitating, the Rebbe opened his drawer, gathered all the money that had been accumulating there for some time and gave it all to him. It amounted to several hundred gold coins.

The man returned home light of heart. Soon the entire city knew about the incident.

R' Yitzchak, the *tzaddik*'s brother, heard about it and disapproved. "What kind of behavior is that?" he grumbled half to himself. "My brother is stingy to a fault when it comes to supporting his own family, but gives away all of his money at a moment's notice to a man who has always been his outspoken opponent!"

Unable to contain his anger, he rushed off to find R' Menachem Mendel. "How could you do that?" he said.

"My dear brother, you are not the first one to condemn my generous act. But just as I ignored the other critic, so will I ignore you. I had good reasons to do what I did."

"Someone was here before me and said the same thing? Who was he?" asked R' Yitzchak.

"It was my *yetzer hara*, my evil inclination. He tried to dissuade me from performing the fine deed that fell into my lap, so to speak. But I overcame his arguments and did what was right!"

On this day the Flood waters were released upon the earth. The Flood annihilated the entire world except for Noach and his family, who were saved inside the Ark and with them, all the species of living things. They came to the Ark, pair by pair, before the Flood.

The Agreement

*W*hen *Hashem* told Noach to take a pair from each species into the Ark, Falsehood came along and wished to enter as well.

"But you cannot enter without a mate," said Noach.

Falsehood went forth to find a mate and met Misfortune. "Would you be willing to be my partner?" he asked.

"What will you give me, if I agree?" asked Misfortune.

"Let us make a deal. Whatever I succeed in gathering will be yours."

Misfortune agreed and the two came before Noach as a pair and were admitted into his Ark.

When they left it, Falsehood went to work and, through his false ways, accumulated considerable profit. Misfortune came and snatched up all Falsehood had gained for himself.

"Why are you seizing my hard-earned gains?" cried Falsehood.

"Don't your remember our agreement?"

Falsehood reluctantly capitulated. And from then on, that bargain has held true. Whatever is gained through falsehood has no permanence, for misfortune comes and wipes out all the profits.

On this day in 5474 (1713), R' Yechezkel Landau, rabbi of Prague, was born. He died on the seventeenth of *Iyar* 5536 (1776). He was the author of the famous *Noda BeYehudah* and other works.

The Long Pesach

R' Yechezkel Landau, rabbi of Prague, was walking home one evening after prayers when he came across a little Christian ragamuffin. The street urchin, dressed in tatters, was carrying two empty baskets and crying as if his heart would break.

The rabbi stopped and turned to the child, "What are you doing in this Jewish neighborhood? And why are you weeping so bitterly?"

The boy was surprised to see a Jew showing concern for a gentile. In his misery, he blurted out his misfortune. "I am a motherless orphan. My father, a baker, sends me out each morning to sell bread. I must sell two basketfuls by night, and, if I do not, my wicked stepmother beats me black and blue."

"And what happened today?" asked the rabbi, kindly.

"Today I was lucky enough to sell all the loaves, but when I wished to return home, I felt in my pocket for the money and saw that it was gone. I had either lost the thirty coins I earned today, or a pickpocket stole them from me.

"If I return home empty handed, my stepmother will whip me mercilessly. I can't bear to think of the pain. Besides, I haven't eaten a thing all day, so why shouldn't I cry?"

A wave of compassion flooded R' Yechezkel's heart and he led the boy to his home, gave him a warm meal, had him rest a while, put thirty coins in his hand and sent him home.

The boy thanked him happily, and went his way.

Many years passed. The gentile child grew up and became a baker, like his father. R' Yechezkel had forgotten about the incident.

One night, on the eve of the eighth day of *Pesach*, after the meal, R' Yechezkel sat alone by his table, studying. It was late; everyone had long gone to sleep. Suddenly, soft footsteps approached the house. He heard a hesitant knock at the door. Wondering who it could be, he went to open it and, to his surprise, found a gentile at his doorstep.

"What are you doing here, so late at night?" he asked in astonishment.

"Shh! Don't you recognize me, rabbi?" he whispered. "I am the gentile orphan whom you found in the streets many, many years ago. You took me into your house, fed me and even gave me money to replace the sum that had been stolen from me."

The rabbi nodded in remembrance and asked, "But what are you doing here, tonight?"

"I have come to repay that kindness. There is a wicked scheme afoot which could be disastrous to your community. I wanted to let you know about it and came here secretly."

He lowered his voice and continued, "It was all my wicked

stepmother's idea. A few days ago, she called a meeting of all the gentile bakers in the city. They conceived a plot to get rid of all the Jews of Prague in one day.

"Each year after your Passover, we gentile bakers bake bread for the Jewish community. (This was permitted by the special ruling of European rabbis.) What easier way to kill you than to put poison in that bread! All the Jews would buy our bread after the holiday and thus, you would all die in one day!

"I heard this evil plan with my own ears. It is being kept a secret by all the bakers, but I decided to let you in on it. I am sure that you will find a way to save the lives of your community. But, please, have mercy on me and don't tell anyone that it was I who divulged the secret to you, or I will pay dearly."

"Many, many thanks!" said R' Yechezkel heartily, but the young baker did not wait to hear his parting words. He was already out the door and had vanished into the night.

R' Yechezkel Landau returned to his room with a heavy heart. No doubt, the youth's words were true. But how could he prevent the calamity? What must he do to foil the bakers' evil plot?

He grappled with the problem for hours on end, trying to find a solution. One thing was clear, it had to remain a secret. But if he could not tell anyone, how could he act?

As the dawn arose, he thought of a plan.

That morning, he sent out speedy messengers to all the synagogues of Prague, ordering the people to attend a special address which he would deliver immediately after the morning service. "The matter is most urgent and affects every single member of our community," he told them. "Everyone is expected to attend."

They came en masse to hear the urgent address. When all had arrived, R' Yechezkel began:"My friends, you all know that with each successive generation, and with the passage of time, more and more Torah is forgotten. Our minds do not have the capacity of those of the ancients. And so it happens that occasionally, a terrible error arises."

The audience opened their eyes wide at this introduction.

"To my regret," he continued, "I must admit that although we are all well versed in the rules governing the Jewish calendar and its Festivals, nevertheless, an error has crept in. It is so grave that it almost caused our community to stumble over the terrible transgression of eating *chametz* on *Pesach*."

People gasped. What a shocking revelation! A miscalculation in the calendar? Eating *chametz* on *Pesach*? How horrible!

"We erred," continued the rabbi, explaining, "this year we began the Festival one day early. According to the true reckoning, today is not the eighth day of *Pesach* but the seventh day ! Tomorrow we must still keep all the laws of *Pesach* as we did this past week. No one must, under any circumstances, eat *chametz* before tomorrow night after dark."

A shaking revelation. No one dared challenge it, though there were scholarly men in the community who were certain that there had been no inaccuracy. There were exact rules, laid down centuries before, and there could have been no mistake. By all their reckoning, *Pesach* should end that very night. But if R' Yechezkel said something, one must heed it without hesitation or protest.

And so, that year the Jews of Prague celebrated *Pesach* for nine days, not the customary eight days of Diaspora communities.

On that ninth day, R' Yechezkel spoke with the chief of police, who sent policemen to all the bakeries. They confiscated all bread baked that day and every loaf contained enough poison to kill anyone who ate only a slice.

A thorough investigation was carried out and the evidence

HaGaon R' Yechezkel Landau, the author of "Noda BeYehudah"

led to the gentile baker responsible for the deed. It was that young lad's father. All the bakers were duly punished.

When the Jews learned about the poisoned bread, they understood what had caused their esteemed rabbi to 'make a mistake' in the calendar, and add a ninth day to the Festival. But they failed to learn how their rabbi had discovered the evil plot.

Several people approached R' Yechezkel and asked him, but he kept his lips sealed.

How, then, did the matter come to light? A short time

before his death, R' Yechezkel Landau told his son, R' Shmuel, the story in detail.

"And do you know why our entire community was saved from certain death?" he said. "Not because of my wisdom, but thanks to the compassion that was aroused in my heart at the sight of the wretched gentile boy. My sympathy prodded me to help him out of his misery and that act of mercy is what spared the Jews of Prague."

R' Shalom Dov of Lubavitch was born on the evening of this day in 5621 (1860) and died on the second of *Nissan*, 5680 (1920). He was the leader of thousands of Chabad chasidim for close to forty years.

The Man and the Leaf

One spring, when R' Shalom Dov of Lubavitch was vacationing in a small resort village, he went out for a walk with his son, R' Yosef Yitzchak. They strolled through the meadows surrounding the village and looked at the grain ripening in the fields. With each puff of wind, the heavily laden stalks swayed to and fro. R' Shalom Dov turned to his son, saying, "Do you see that? Just think, every single motion of a wheat stalk, every bending of a blade of grass is a separate act of Divine Providence!"

HaAdmur R' Shalom of Lubavitch

They walked on until they reached the woods. It was cool and refreshing and they continued on, meandering through the trees. R' Yosef Yitzchak was contemplating the profound concept that his father had just uttered, that every motion of each blade of grass revealed a specific act of Providence.

He was so wrapped up in his thoughts that, while passing under a tree, he absent-mindedly tore off a leaf and rolled it unconsciously between his fingers. As they continued, he shredded it and threw the pieces underfoot without realizing what he was doing.

His father noticed the destructive act and turned to his son. "How can you treat a creation of the Almighty so callously?" he said. "We just spoke about Divine Providence embracing every living thing and you unfeelingly sever a leaf from its source of life, the tree. Don't you know that the tree was created for a definite purpose? It is alive; it breathes. Not only did you pluck that leaf from its source but you cruelly tore it to bits and threw it underfoot like a worthless object. Why is that leaf different from you? True, man is on a higher rung of Creation than the plant, but just as you have a purpose to fulfill on earth, so does the leaf. And both of you, leaf and man, reflect the profound design of the Creator."

20 Cheshvan

R' Avraham Yaakov of Sadigura, the leader of thousands of Sadigura chasidim, was born on this day in 5580 (1819). He died on the eleventh of *Elul*, 5643 (1883).

Tribulation and Succor

When R' Yisrael of Ruzhin lived in Russia, the government made false accusations against him, seized him and threw him into prison. He suffered greatly there, but, finally, succeeded in escaping together with his family. He crossed the Russian border and reached Sadigur, Austria. The Austrian government granted him asylum.

R' Yisrael died outside of Russia, but the Russian government continued to hound his descendants, the Ruzhiner dynasty, on the grounds that they were a subversive and dangerous element.

The Russian government was aided by Jewish informers, the *maskilim*. The *maskilim* resented the fact that R' Avraham Yaakov of Sadigur, son and successor of R' Yisrael, made his center in the Austrian city, for they viewed Austria as their stronghold. They knew that the Rebbe would fight them with all his might and arrest the spread of their influence. Together, they plotted against the Rebbe and the Austrian authorities cast him into jail.

❀ ❀ ❀

The warden of the jail where R' Avraham Yaakov was imprisoned was a notorious anti-Semite. He gloated over the opportunity of having this noted Jew in his clutches and wanted to inflict as much suffering upon him as his devious mind could conceive.

His first step was to throw him into a cell together with a hardened criminal, who was a rabid anti-Semite. This prisoner would be sure to render the Rebbe's life in prison doubly unbearable.

The chasidim toiled tirelessly to free their leader and, at least, to improve his condition until he was released. They were finally allowed to bring a comfortable couch into the cell.

The other prisoner seethed with envy at the sight of this piece of furniture in their tiny cell. Would a Jew be allowed to rest comfortably while he, a gentile, had to sleep on a hard prison cot? "It shall not be!" he swore. "Not as long as I am here!" He slashed a deep cross into the couch's upholstery.

When the Rebbe saw the cross, he refused to lie or sit on the sofa. He stood on his feet all day while his cellmate, the gentile, stretched himself out at leisure upon it.

This was not the only bothersome thing that plagued the Rebbe during his imprisonment. Near the prison was a monastery. Church bells rang every hour, on the hour, and the priests could be heard at their prayers. The Rebbe could not bear to hear the impure sound and pressed his fingertips deep into his ears to shut it out.

Thus he stood all day, for many days, on his feet, his fingers plugging up his ears, reciting *Tehillim* by heart.

This ordeal was to leave its mark on the Rebbe's health for many years to come. His hearing would suffer and his ears would pain him greatly. His feet were never to recover either.

The Rebbe suffered excruciatingly, but he never uttered a word of complaint, not about the ringing bells, nor about his cellmate who had marred the couch. He resigned himself to his fate and did not stop praying.

The sight of the holy man praying to his Creator with such adherence infuriated his cellmate even further. The man was silent, at first, but then rose from the comfortable couch he had appropriated and disturbed the Rebbe at his prayers. He became so unruly that R' Avraham Yaakov was unable to concentrate and had to stop praying. It was then that he complained to the prison warden.

The anti-Semitic warden ignored the complaint and secretly congratulated the criminal for successfully disturbing the Jew.

The criminal's self-confidence rose with the warden's encouragement and he intensified his harassment.

A few days passed thus, the gentile doing his utmost to make the Rebbe's life unbearable and the warden urging him on behind the scenes. The Rebbe bore his suffering in silence, exhibiting supernatural self-control.

One day, R' Avraham Yaakov attempted to pray despite his neighbor. The man began his disturbance and then, with a

Beis Medrash of the Admur of Sadigura

sudden cry, he fell to the ground, writhing in pain. "Help! Help!" he screamed.

The guards rushed to the cell to see what was the matter. The warden came, too, and bent over him to hear what he was trying to say. The criminal was murmuring weakly, "Take me out of here, quickly. If I remain in here any longer, I will die."

The guards looked at the warden questioningly when, he, too, slumped to the ground in pain. His fearful shrieks mingled with those of the prisoner.

The guards intuitively understood that this was Heavenly retribution. These two men, who had tortured the holy rabbi, were being punished for their wickedness.

They quickly dragged the two suffering men out of the cell. Only when assurances were given that the Rebbe was to be left alone, did their pains subside.

From that day on, the prison inmates knew that the Rebbe was a godly and exalted man and all feared him. He was treated with the utmost respect until the day of his release.

R' David Shlomo Eibshitz passed away in Tzefas on the evening of this day in 5670 (1909). One of the great leaders of Chasidus, he wrote *"Levushei Serad"* and *"Arvei Nachal."*

Two Rooms

The home of R' David Shlomo Eibshitz had two rooms for the hearing of judicial cases.

He and his fellow judges sat in one room, while the two litigants sat in the other and presented their pleas.

Thus, R' David Shlomo never knew who was the defendant and who the plaintiff. And so, he was able to issue his halachic rulings without the least hint of favoritism.

R' Yissachar Dov of Belz passed away on this day in 5687 (1926) at the age of seventy-four. R' Yissachar Dov was one of the foremost Chasidic figures of his generation and the leader of the thousands of Belzer chasidim.

The Note and the Sigh

When Mordechai (later known as R' Mordechai of Bilgoray), the son of the Belzer Rebbe, reached military age and was called up before the draft board, he wrote a *kvittel* note and brought it to his father, begging that he pray for his exemption from the army.

The Rebbe opened the folded piece of paper. When he read its contents, he heaved a bitter sigh, a sigh so loud that it reached the *rebbetzin's* ears and threw her into confusion. What had the Rebbe seen in his holy vision? Did the sigh mean, Heaven forbid, that their son would not be exempted?

She rushed to her husband and said, "Hundreds of young men have been saved through your prayers and were freed from military duty. Why is our son's case different? Is it more difficult for you to plead for him, that you sigh so? Pray for him as you do for the rest!"

"That was not why I sighed," replied the *tzaddik*. "When I

HaAdmur R' Yissachar Dov of Belz

read my son's note, I feared that his plight affected me more than did that of other young men in his position. It is because I took greater interest in his welfare than in theirs that I sighed."

In Heaven, on Earth, and Under the Earth

R' Yissachar Dov once took a long train trip in which the route passed through an underground tunnel. He anticipated that part of the journey and asked often when they would reach the tunnel.

His companions were curious and watched the Rebbe carefully when they finally did enter the tunnel. R' Yissachar Dov sank into deep thought and recited the *Shema*.

Later, when the chasidim asked why he had done so, he explained, "The Almighty rules in Heaven, on earth and even under the earth. In Heaven, the angels and *seraphim* crown Him as King; on earth, we, Jews, establish Him as our King. But who is there to acknowledge His rule under the earth? I was now given the opportunity to do just that. When the train crossed through the underground passage, I recited the *Shema* to declare my subservience to the Kingdom of *Hashem* even under the ground."

This used to be celebrated as a festive day, for on this day the Jews demolished the building which the gentiles had erected in the courtyard of the *Beis Hamikdash*. Since the *churban* (destruction), our synagogues and study halls (*batei midrashos*) have served us as a *mikdash m'at*, a miniature Temple. In the past, we have often had to fight for the existence and preservation of these sacred structures.

Matzos Before and After

When R' Shalom of Belz was about to erect his grand synagogue, the wealthy squire of the entire area which included the city of Belz, decided, out of spite, to build a church directly opposite. "I am a second Haman!" he declared.

When the Rebbe was told what the landowner had said, he replied, "Tell him that his downfall will be like Haman's."

Once, when the *tzaddik* was on his way to the synagogue, he was accosted by the landowner's son who came towards him with a slice of pork. "Sir, this is for you to eat," he said arrogantly.

The moment the words left his mouth, he began to suffer convulsions. His limbs shook violently and he lost control over them. The landlord rushed over to the Rebbe, shouting,

"Forgive him! Save my son!" The Rebbe refused, and the son died.

This made the landowner hate the Jews all the more. He sought countless new ways to persecute the Rebbe and make his life miserable.

When it was finally completed, the synagogue stood tall and proud, towering above all the homes in Belz and also over the church across the street. When the landowner saw this, he decided that his church, which had not yet been completed, must be higher still. But the Rebbe said confidently, "He will not be victorious over me. With the help of *Hashem*, he will never finish that building."

Within a short while, it became known that the lot upon which the church was being constructed did not even belong to the man. It was the property of orphans and had been illegally appropriated by the landowner. The courts stepped in and ordered it sold at a public auction.

The gentile knew that the Jews would bid against him and would be willing to pay an astronomical price just to make sure that he did not acquire it. And so he threatened, "If any Jew dares bid for this land, I will have him killed."

R' Shalom found a way to overcome this obstacle. He contacted an admirer of his, a gentile Viennese doctor, and begged him to attend the auction and bid on behalf of the Jewish community. He authorized him to raise the price to any amount necessary.

The doctor came and bought the land without the landowner daring to harm him. The rabbi demolished the church and built various communal structures upon it.

The landowner would still not admit defeat. While he had failed to erect a church on this street, he could try again on another one. He found a plot that also overlooked the synagogue and began construction there. "This time I will build a church higher than the synagogue," he boasted.

Pesach was approaching. The landowner, the authority in Belz, issued a new law forbidding the baking of *matzah* under the pretense that it was a fire hazard.

His decree did not frighten R' Shalom. On the contrary, it fit in with his plans. Each year, the Rebbe would send his chasidim to nearby villages and towns for *Pesach*, since feeding such a large group was too burdensome for his family. That year, however, he told the followers to remain in Belz, despite the new ordinance. "I trust in *Hashem* that there will be enough *matzos* for all and plenty to spare."

And so it was. A few days after the order was issued, the landowner was riding his horse along a narrow path when the count from a neighboring estate appeared from the opposite direction. The road was too narrow for them to pass each other, but neither man would concede the right of way. A fight broke out. Their honor was now at stake. The count drew his pistol and killed the landowner of Belz.

The Jews of Belz exulted when they heard the news. And that year, as the Rebbe had predicted, there were *matzos* in plenty.

R' Refael Hakohen, rabbi of Hamburg, was born on this day in 5483 (1722). He was one of the great *poskim* of our people and author of *Toras Yekusiel*. He died on the twenty-sixth of *Cheshvan* in 5564 (1803).

The Endorsement

*W*hen R' Refael Hakohen was asked to serve as rabbi of the illustrious community of Hamburg, Germany, he traveled there to get acquainted with the congregation.

Winds of the Enlightenment movement were then blowing through the cities of Germany and many of the dignitaries in the community were strongly influenced by the philosophy of Mendelssohn, head of the Enlightenment in Berlin, who reared his head in defiance of Jewish tradition.

The Enlightenment was an unknown entity to R' Refael, who came from Lithuania, where such influences had not yet penetrated into the vineyard of *Hashem*. People were, as yet, unaware of the existence of such a movement. Thus, when several prominent men of the community, who secretly leaned towards the *Haskalah*, approached him with a suggestion, he did not grasp its implication. "If you would like to be appointed as rabbi of the illustrious confederation of the A.H.W.

communities (Altona, Hamburg and Wandsbak)," they told him, "you had best go to Berlin and receive a letter of recommendation from the great sage, Moshe Mendelssohn. His endorsement will open all doors to you with ease."

Following their counsel, R' Refael innocently traveled to Berlin, the city where the buds of Enlightenment had first appeared. While he was en route, the prominent men in Hamburg sent an express letter to Mendelssohn, stating: "A Lithuanian rabbi by the name of R' Refael Hakohen is about to reach you. We ask you to interview him and tell us if you think he is suited to be the rabbi of a fashionable, sophisticated community such as we strive to be."

When R' Refael arrived in Berlin, he sought out Mendelssohn's home at once. He was shocked to find him studying *Tanach* bare headed! This was too much for R' Refael. Was this the man whose endorsement he had been told to seek?

R' Refael stood there horrified, his limbs frozen, his heart beating furiously.

Mendelssohn raised his head and looked at the rabbi. "*Shalom aleichem*, peace unto you," he greeted him courteously.

His words broke the spell. R' Refael exploded with the verse, "There is no peace, says *Hashem*, for the wicked." And then, the pain in his heart welled up and burst forth. "What did they do to me? Did they truly send me to this *apikorus* (heretic) for a letter of recommendation to serve as rabbi? I would rather clean sewers; I would gladly go begging from door to door; I prefer to live a life of deprivation and suffering rather than to have to degrade myself by asking the likes of you for a good word!" And with this, he stormed out, embittered and shaken, and returned to Hamburg.

Before he arrived, the same dignitaries in Hamburg received Mendelssohn's reply. Interestingly enough, he wrote:

"I did not get a chance to become acquainted with the candidate you sent me. As soon as he saw me studying *Tanach* without a headcovering, he lashed into me and called me an *apikorus*. He refused to accept any endorsement. And for this very reason, I am inclined to advise you to accept him as your rabbi. He is a man of integrity. A man of his caliber will not be partial to anyone, not even if a sword point be thrust at his throat."

R' Refael was, indeed, crowned as rabbi of the A.H.W. federation. During his tenure, he fought the Enlightenment tooth and nail, giving no quarter. But those same Jews who had sent him to Mendelssohn fought him every inch of the way and embittered his life. In the end, he could not bear the strife and resigned.

R' Refael's last years were filled with pain and suffering. Yet, the Torah continued to be his guiding light and he did not waver from the truth to the very end.

The cities of Samaria, in *Eretz Yisrael*, were fortified with formidable stone walls. Their construction was completed during the period of the second *Beis Hamikdash* on this date. It was considered as a *yom tov*. Then, as now, the gentiles harassed Jewish settlements, but *Hashem* protected His people through numerous miracles.

The Governor's Downfall

*T*he ruler of Tzefas was an evil despot by nature, and a rabid anti-Semite, besides. The Turkish government empowered him with limitless authority. He could even, if he so wished, capriciously put people to death. With such a free hand, it was small wonder that he made the lives of his Jewish subjects miserable, by issuing oppressive decrees left and right.

Once, he demanded that the Jewish community give him an exorbitant sum within five weeks. If the Jews were to be even one day late, they would be expelled from the city or, perhaps, even put to death.

The Jews were thrown into a turmoil. "What shall we do?" they asked one another frantically. "How will we ever raise such an enormous sum? We are all poor, as it is!" And they knew the governor had not made an empty threat. He could be relied on to drive them out, or possibly, put them to death.

They gathered to discuss the problem and seek a solution. Finally, they came to a decision: The heads of the community would travel to Constantinople where the sultan resided and pour out their tale of woe in his ears. "Since he is the governor's superior, he can overrule him and annul the decree," they said. "Perhaps he will show mercy towards us!"

"We must include the *shammash* in the delegation," one man reminded the rest. "He is a holy man and capable of performing miracles."

A committee was soon formed which included the *shammash*, R' Elazar Azkari, author of *Sefer Hacharedim*.

When the group reached the port of Acco, the *shammash* said to the others, "I advise you all to return home to Tzefas. I will continue on to Constantinople alone. With your prayers to accompany me, I will, please G-d, succeed in my mission."

They knew that R' Elazar was a saintly man and followed his counsel; they all returned home, wishing him good fortune in his endeavor. R' Elazar remained at the port. He found a ship bound for Turkey, but as the sea was becalmed, it had not been able to embark on the journey.

Soon after R' Elazar boarded, a stiff wind arose and the ship set sail. It was an easterly wind of such force that the ship was borne as if on wings. That very day, to the surprise of the captain and his seasoned sailors, they docked at the port of Constantinople, having covered a distance which, under the best of conditions, took several days and at times, weeks.

The passengers were overjoyed to have reached their destination so quickly, and praised *Hashem* Who had wrought the miracle.

R' Elazar Azkari debarked and set out for the city. He found the *shammash* of the local synagogue and asked if he could lodge with him. "Gladly," he replied, "but as you can see, my humble home is barely enough for my large family. Where could I put up such a distinguished guest as yourself?"

"Do you have a small shed or loft? That would suit me fine," suggested R' Elazar.

"If you do not object, you can use our tiny attic," said the shammash. He prepared a bed and set a candle on the table. R' Elazar secluded himself in the small room with his sefarim and began studying. When midnight struck, he recited the tikkun chatzos and afterwards continued studying, just as he did each night in his home in Tzefas.

That night, in which R' Elazar was absorbed in Torah, was a sleepless one for the sultan, as well. His daughter suddenly took ill. She was convulsed with pain, but the best doctors could do nothing to ease it. The sultan was beside himself with worry, for she seemed on the brink of death.

He paced his room restlessly, back and forth, trying to find some peace for his soul. The hours passed and still he stalked about like a caged lion. And in his pacing, he approached a window for a breath of fresh air.

He looked down upon the houses nestling on the mountain slope, and envied his subjects their peaceful slumber. "How fortunate they are to be able to sleep," he mused. His glance swept across the scene and was drawn to a bright light.

"Fire!" he exclaimed, and ran off to awaken a servant.

"There seems to be a fire down in the city. Go down to investigate and sound the alarm, if need be, before the fire spreads."

The servants left the palace in the middle of the night and went towards the light.

They came to the ramshackle cottage of the shammash and pounded on the door. The shammash answered sleepily, but came awake with a start when he saw the sultan's men on his threshold. His heart pounded. "What is the matter?" he asked fearfully.

"The sultan saw a light here from his window," they explained. "He was fearful lest a fire had broken out and sent us here to investigate. Show us the way to the attic."

"Strange," they murmured as they walked up the flight of stairs. "There is no smoke and no smell of fire."

They reached the attic and found R' Elazar Azkari seated at the table, studying by candlelight.

"It is nothing more than one small candle," they exclaimed in surprise. "Was this the great light our master saw far off in his palace?"

They returned to report to the sultan. "We saw no fire and no great light," they said, "only a Jew studying by a single candle."

"How strange," said the sultan. "At this very moment, I see a brilliant glow surrounding that attic. It must be significant. Go back and fetch the Jew."

Before long, R' Elazar was standing in the sultan's chamber. The sultan had only to gaze upon him to realize that he was a great and saintly man. He decided to speak to R' Elazar of his anguish. "My daughter took ill this night and seems to be dying," he told the rabbi. "The doctors are helpless to cure her and have given up hope. Perhaps you, a holy man, can help us. How can we save my poor daughter from death?"

"With the help of the Almighty, I will heal her," promised R' Elazar. He retired to a corner of the room and, shutting his eyes tightly, prayed fervently, "O, Healer of all flesh, send a speedy recovery to the sultan's daughter."

A servant rushed breathlessly into the room. "Your Majesty, the princess just opened her eyes and smiled. She seems to have passed the crisis!"

R' Elazar remained in the sultan's palace for the next day. To the amazement of all the court physicians, the princess improved from hour to hour. Her rapid recovery mystified them. This could only be due to the rabbi and his prayers!

By nightfall, the princess had completely recovered. The sultan gazed lovingly at his daughter, his heart full of gratitude. Turning to the rabbi, he said, "How can I thank you? I owe my daughter's life to you. Ask what you will, and your wish shall be granted."

R' Elazar told the sultan of the troubles of the Tzefas community. He told of the oppression they had suffered for years at the hands of the tyrannical governor and of the new demand he had imposed upon them. "We have already been milked dry by taxes and would never be able to gather even a tenth of the necessary amount. Our suffering has reached the limit; we can bear it no longer. The governor knows that we will be unable to produce the money. He hates us and is looking for an excuse to banish or kill us. Your Majesty, please save us."

The sultan listened intently, his expression hardening with suppressed rage. "Do not worry," he said. "That governor will oppress you no longer. I will depose him and install you as the new ruler!"

"But, Your Majesty, that is unnecessary. I am not seeking power for myself; I am not fit to be governor. All I ask is that you appoint a new one, a kindly official. Charge him to treat your Jewish subjects fairly and not to issue any decrees before consulting me and receiving my permission."

"Very well," said the sultan.

"I would like Your Majesty to record this in writing and seal it with your royal seal," added R' Elazar.

"That shall be done, too," agreed the sultan. He wrote a letter to the governor of Tzefas informing him that a new ruler would soon be appointed. "Meanwhile, you are not to demand money from the Jews or pass any decrees large or small without the express knowledge and permission of the bearer of this letter."

Armed with this important document and laden down with

money and many costly gifts, R' Elazar left Constantinople and sailed for the shores of his home, *Eretz Yisrael*.

The Jews of Tzefas were overjoyed with the news of his success. The leaders of the community met and decided to take no action until the payment fell due. The governor would surely send an official to fetch the money. "We will tell him that the *shammash* has it," they said.

The appointed day arrived. The governor, as expected, sent an official to collect the money. "My master said that he would not extend the period and wants the entire sum at once," declared the messenger.

"The money is to be found with R' Elazar Azkari," said the leaders of the community.

When the governor heard this, he flew into a rage. "They are putting me off with flimsy excuses! But I will show them that I mean business! I will give them a taste of my mighty arm!" He stormed off towards the *shammash*'s home.

He barged in, expecting the *shammash* to cringe and grovel before him. But R' Elazar did not even budge from his seat. This infuriated the governor even more. "Where is the money?" he shouted menacingly.

The *shammash* rose and began rummaging leisurely among his things, as if searching for the money. But he was looking for the sultan's letter.

He found it and handed it to the governor, whose eyes bulged at the sign of the royal seal. He opened it up with trepidation and read. His heart sank. A few moments before, he had been on top of the world, a powerful ruler about to receive an enormous sum of money. And now, not only had the dream of money faded before his eyes, but even his position was no longer his. And to compound his downfall, he had to suffer the degradation of having to obey this Jew who stood before him.

He fell to R' Elazar's feet and pleaded tearfully, "Please

forgive me! Forgive me!" But nothing could change things, now. The decree had already been sealed by the sultan's hand and had become law.

It was a bitter defeat for the cruel governor and a joyous victory for the Jews of Tzefas. They celebrated the great miracle that *Hashem* had wrought and thanked Him with all their hearts (*from 'Shem Hagedolim' of the Chida*).

26 Cheshvan

This is the tenth day of the Flood. The generation of the Flood was sentenced to annihilation in the year 1656 after Creation (2104 B.C.E.) for the sin of robbery.

The Wonder Horse

R' Yehoshua Heshel Milner lived in Jerusalem over a century ago. A devout and learned man, he derived his income from a flour mill which had shifts around the clock. R' Yehoshua Heshel rarely visited the mill, however, since he employed an efficient manager, Shmuel, whom he trusted. Shmuel ran things smoothly, to his satisfaction, leaving the owner free to study Torah.

These were the days before the discovery of electricity. R' Yehoshua Heshel's mill was not situated near a river, and had to be operated on horse power. A horse was harnessed to the immense upper millstone and as it walked around and around, the stone revolved, grinding the kernels placed on the fixed lower millstone. To prevent the horse, which walked in the unstopping circles, from getting dizzy, a blindfold was tied about its eyes and thus, unaware of the circular movement, it could plod on for a lengthy stretch of time.

Shmuel died and R' Yehoshua Heshel replaced him with another capable manager. Shortly thereafter, the mill acquired a new horse. It was a magnificent beast, healthy, massive and powerful and worked so diligently that within minutes, it could accomplish that which other horses did in several hours.

Word got out about this wonder horse. "A horse like that is being wasted at the mill," people said. "With such muscles, it should be pulling heavy loads or transporting people great distances. It is being wasted on such common work."

Indeed, porters and wagon drivers set their eyes on the powerful mill horse and approached R' Yehoshua Heshel to sell the animal.

At first, he ignored their offers, but when the bids increased in amount and frequency, he set a price of twenty-five napoleons and waited for a buyer willing to pay such an astronomical sum. (An average family, for example, could subsist on one napoleon for an entire month!)

But that enormous sum did not deter those truly interested in buying the horse. Finally, one Jerusalem merchant came to terms with R' Yehoshua Heshel and they set a date to enact the transaction.

On the night before the sale, R' Yehoshua Heshel tossed and turned restlessly in bed. He finally arose, dressed and left the house. "I'll be back soon," he told his family, who wondered where he was going at such a late hour.

With long strides, he made his way to the mill. His employees were surprised to see him in the middle of the night, for he rarely came at all. "What is the matter?" they asked.

R' Yehoshua Heshel brushed their questions aside and went straight to the horse. He whispered in its ear, "Shmuel, I forgive you. Do you hear, Shmuel? I forgive you wholeheartedly."

As soon as the horse heard these words, it fell to the ground and died. R' Yehoshua Heshel left the mill and returned home.

The next morning, the city reeled from the news. The mill owner's wonder horse, which had been slated for sale that very day, had suddenly collapsed and died the night before! A healthy horse in its prime, for no apparent reason!

R' Yehoshua Heshel gathered his family and friends and explained the matter. "Last night I could not sleep. I finally dozed off fitfully and had a strange dream. My former manager, Shmuel, appeared to me and said, 'I want you to know that I am really your wonder horse.' I looked at him unbelievingly. He burst into tears and confessed, 'I was not the perfect manager you thought me to be. I betrayed your trust and stole from the profits all through the years. After I died and came before the Heavenly court, I was sentenced to return to earth in the form of a horse and to work off my debt to you at the mill. I was given a powerful build so that I could work doubly hard and settle my account with you through excellent labor. But now that you are about to sell me, I will not be able to work for you and will have to descend to earth once more, for I have not as yet paid up my debt. I cannot bear the thought of returning once again. I would rather burn in *gehinnom*. Please, have pity on me. Find it in your heart to forgive my sin.'

"My heart went out to him. I got up, hurried off to the mill and whispered in the horse's ear that I truly forgave him. Having received my word of pardon, his purpose on earth was fulfilled and so, he died. Poor Shmuel; now, at last, his soul will rest in peace."

In ancient days, this day was celebrated as a festival to commemorate a miracle. A delay in the sacrifice of the daily offering in the *Beis Hamikdash* was successfully prevented.

The Pure and the Impure

R' Yisrael, the *Maggid* of Kozhnitz, was a small boy when people noted his spark of greatness. One morning, after he had recited the *eizehu mekoman* section in the prayers, he turned to his teacher and asked, "Why are the sacrifices of atonement eaten within the confines of the *Beis Hamikdash*, while the sacrifices which are brought voluntarily may be eaten anywhere in the city? I would think that the reverse should be true: The voluntary sacrifices were brought with a pure heart and noble intentions and should be eaten in a holy place, whereas the sin-offerings are brought as atonement for impure deeds and should be eaten anywhere but in the holy *Beis Hamikdash*."

Yisrael ventured to answer his own question: "But, actually, it is not so. A person who has sinned needs to be watchful and cautious, lest he sin again. He, especially, needs the protective holy atmosphere of the *Beis Hamikdash*, for if he ate his sacrifice anywhere in the city, he might be tempted to go astray once more. The person who brought a voluntary offering, on the other hand, is on a high spiritual level to begin with and is not in danger of slipping. He, therefore, can eat his offering anywhere in the city without fear of being harmfully influenced by its atmosphere."

We hope and pray for rain in *Eretz Yisrael* during these days.

The Two Princesses

In the time of the holy *tanaim*, R' Eliezer and R' Akiva, there was a severe drought.

R' Eliezer declared a public fast. Everyone gathered to pray, but no rain fell.

R' Akiva, then, also declared a day of fasting and prayer. The people filled the synagogues, prayed, and were answered with blessed rain.

When R' Akiva saw this, he feared that R' Eliezer might berate himself. He, therefore, gathered the people and spoke: "To what can this be compared? To a king who had two daughters. One was an arrogant shrew and the other, a sweet, modest girl. Whenever the oldest daughter, the shrew, came to her father with a demand, he would tell his servants to fulfill it at once. 'Just get rid of her as quickly as possible,' he would say. But if his winsome daughter came, he would engage her in conversation and detain her as long as he could, so charmed was he by her company. Only after a long stay would he, finally, carry out her wish."

The people smiled at the comparison but understood R' Akiva's point. They continued to revere both of the Sages equally, as in the past (*Yerushalmi, Taanis, Chap. 3*).

R' Naftali Tzvi Yehudah Berlin, known as the Netziv, was born on this day in 5577 (1816). He was the *rosh yeshivah* of Volozhin and was esteemed as a holy and learned man. He died on the twenty-eighth of *Av* in 5653 (1893).

The Donor's Due

The Netziv of Volozhin once sent two men out to raise money for the *yeshivah*. They were to travel to towns and villages and solicit donations from Jews everywhere.

And so their journey began. At their first stop, before they had even approached anyone, one of them had an interesting idea.

"Why must we exert ourselves with exhausting travels, when our work could be made so much easier by buying a

R' Naftali Tzvi Yehudah Berlin — the Netziv of Lublin

lottery ticket? Then, all we have to do is pray for our number and wait for the drawing. Nothing could be simpler."

"You know," said the other, "you are right. And your idea makes good sense, too. After all, the same One Who implants the idea in the minds of people to donate to the *yeshivah* can surely make our ticket win. I suggest we buy ticket number 2118 and then pray for success."

"Fine, then it is decided. You buy the ticket and I will go to the synagogue to pray."

One went off to purchase the ticket. But on the way, he toyed around with the number and thought, "Why did I say number 2118 when the one before, 2117, is the exact numerical count of *'ach tov* — only good'? I will buy that number, instead." And so he did.

Meanwhile, the other *shaliach* went to the synagogue. He settled in a corner and prayed fervently that number 2118 win. He prayed with all his heart and soul, and Heaven answered his prayer. Number 2118 drew the grand prize.

Imagine how the two men felt when they learned that they had missed by a hairsbreadth — and through their own doing! They hurried back to Volozhin to tell the Netziv the sad news.

The Netziv listened to their tale, then asked, "Do you really think that the Almighty, Who provides for and sustains the entire world and all its creatures, cannot provide the *yeshivah*'s needs without your exertion and bother? Don't you think that if He wished, He could supply the necessary funds in a twinkling of an eye? However, *Hashem* wishes to improve His people by giving them *mitzvos* to fulfill. He wishes that many Jews be involved in maintaining the learning of Torah. When you travel to outlying villages and remote settlements, you offer countless Jews the opportunity of sharing in the study of Torah, even if they, themselves, are unlearned. The Torah is their heritage, too, and through their support, they have a portion in it. You two sought the easy way out, thus denying these Jews their birthright. But you did not get your way. Providence willed it otherwise, and you will have to travel to solicit their help after all, if not for the *yeshivah*'s sake, then for theirs."

First Day of Rosh Chodesh Kislev

R' Tzvi Hirsh of Riminov passed away on this day in 5607 (1846). R' Tzvi Hirsh first served as the *shammash* of his master, R' Menachem Mendel of Riminov, but upon the Rebbe's death, was chosen to wear his mantle of leadership.

The Shammash-Rebbe

When R' Tzvi Hirsh was the *shammash* of the Rebbe of Riminov, his greatness was recognized by R' Naftali of Ropshitz. He appreciated the exalted soul resting within him and foresaw the illustrious future awaiting him.

R' Naftali once turned to R' Menachem Mendel and said, "I would never agree to have such a *ganav* (thief) as my personal attendant and allow him the run of my house. Why, you never know, he might turn about and steal anything he finds here, including your Torah knowledge and piety, your Divine intuition and your followers."

R' Menachem Mendel smiled at the comparison and said, "I am glad to be able to fulfill the verse, 'One who walks the straightforward road, he will serve me.' Besides, I am confident that as long as I am still alive, he will not usurp my power or 'steal' anything of mine."

R' Naftali was the only one among the many disciples who saw beyond the humble exterior. The other chasidim belittled R' Tzvi Hirsh and looked down upon him. This attitude changed only, when they saw the Rebbe treating him with respect. Their disdain actually turned to admiration, when the Rebbe once said, "Whoever insults 'my R' Hirsh' must make sure to appease him."

It all came about thus.

Each *erev Rosh Chodesh*, the day known as the *Yom Kippur Kattanr*, R' Menachem Mendel would send out a small committee composed of the *shammash* and a few other trusted chasidim to inspect the weights and measures of the community. They would go to all the shops in Riminov and later, report back to the Rebbe.

"A rabbi of a city is required to see to the accuracy of the weights and measures even more than he is obligated to inspect the knives of the slaughterers," R' Menachem Mendel would often say.

Once, the committee entered the shop of a wealthy and scholarly Jew. In his shop, of all places, they found a faulty weight.

"This weight is inaccurate," said R' Tzvi Hirsh. "You must not use it."

"Don't you think I know that? We don't use it!"

"But even if you don't use it, you are not permitted to leave it about. The Talmud says that one must not have a faulty measure in his home, even if he uses it for the most insignificant or degrading purpose (*Bava Basra 89b*)."

The shopkeeper snickered and said snidely, "Well, well, look who has become our new halachic authority! The *shammash*, himself, no less!"

R' Tzvi Hirsh did not reply. He lowered his head, trying to conceal the tears of shame that formed in his eyes.

That day, when the committee returned to the Rebbe and

was asked about their inspection, the *shammash* said, "Thank G-d, the Jewish people are a worthy nation. All their weights and measures were in order. Nothing was amiss." He chose to ignore the incident in which he had been treated so degradingly.

Not so his companions. When R' Tzvi Hirsh left the room, one man spoke up and told the Rebbe exactly what had happened.

When R' Menachem Mendel heard this, he summoned a chasid and said, "Take a gavel and go from house to house. Knock at the doors and tell the people to come to an emergency meeting. Make sure to notify everyone, except for the guilty shopkeeper."

Before long, all the Jews of Riminov had assembled in the synagogue. What urgent message did the rabbi have to impart?

The speech was devoted to the importance of accurate weights and measures. The Rebbe described what had happened that day and said, "And when 'my R' Hirsh' told the shopkeeper that he must not leave such a weight lying about, the man mocked him."

When the missing shopkeeper heard that the Rebbe had singled him out, he hurried to him and pleaded, "Forgive me! I didn't realize . . ."

"I will forgive you on condition that you donate fifty gold coins to the poor of Riminov," said the Rebbe. The guilty man agreed without a murmur.

"You abused R' Tzvi Hirsh, my *shammash*, and questioned his learning," said the Rebbe. "I will have you know that I doubt whether the teacher who taught you Torah, Talmud and *poskim* knows as much as R' Tzvi Hirsh!"

When the *shammash* heard that his master had made a public revelation of the story, he wept and his lips murmured a silent prayer.

"Why did you weep and what did you pray for?" he was asked.

"I prayed that Heaven not punish the shopkeeper, before he had the chance to set the Rebbe's mind at peace ..."